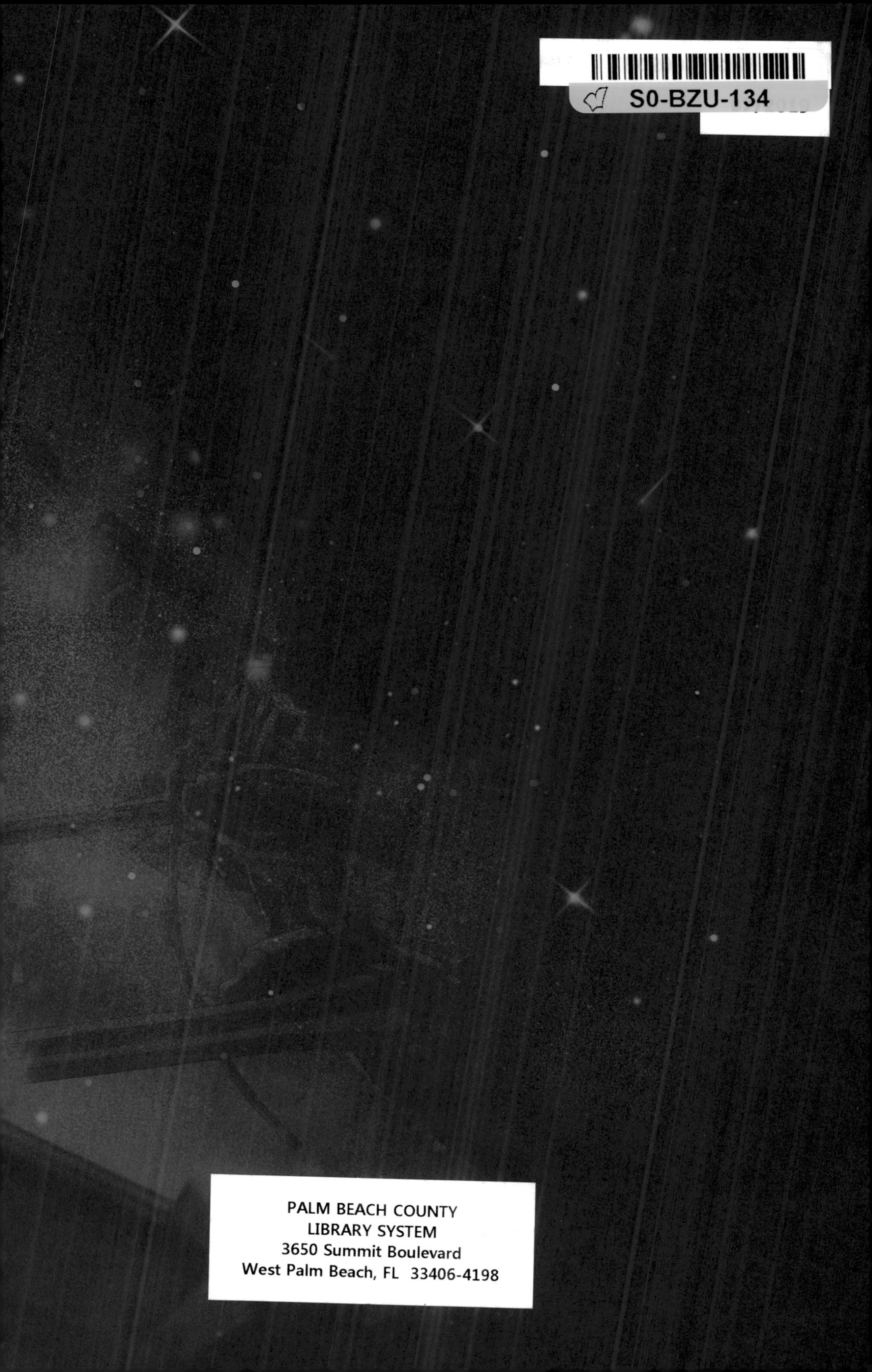

LEGENDARY
COMICS

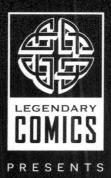

PRESENTS

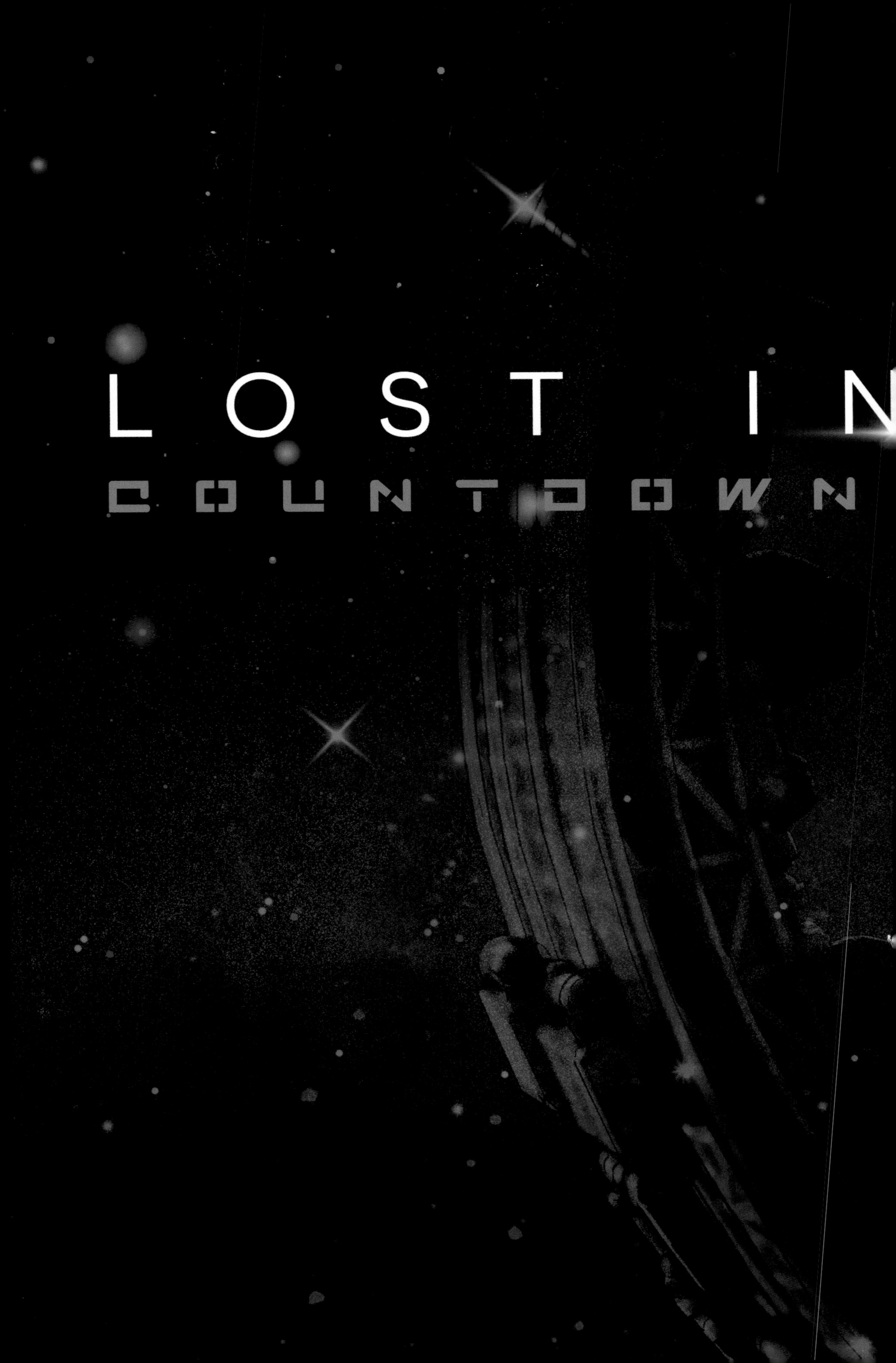
LOST IN
COUNTDOWN

S P A C E
DANGER

WRITERS
RICHARD DINNICK   **BRIAN BUCCELLATO**
"Secrets"   "Penny & Judith"

ART
ZID

COLOR ASSISTS
SYNCRAFT STUDIO

STORY CONSULTANTS
DEREK THIELGES
KEVIN BURNS
JON JASHNI

LETTERING AND DESIGN
JOHN ROSHELL & SARAH JACOBS
of COMICRAFT

EDITOR
ROBERT NAPTON

SPECIAL THANKS
ZACK ESTRIN
MATT SAZAMA
BURK SHARPLESS
EDWIN CHUNG
SONIA BORRIS
MAUREEN MURPHY
OMAR KHAN
THE CAST AND CREW OF LOST IN SPACE

"Secrets"

With the Earth a toxic mess and her marriage seemingly over, Professor **Maureen Robinson** decides to take her children (**Judy, Penny** and **Will**) off-world to the colony on Alpha Centauri to start a new life. But then her special forces husband, **John**, finds out and decides to go with them.

That's not her only problem. During the rigorous training they all had to undergo, Will failed one of the tests. Desperate, Maureen was forced to do whatever it took to get him on the colony ship The Resolute - paying for someone to falsify his test scores.

But she is not the only one looking for a new life. Scam artist **June Harris** has drugged her sister, **Jessica**, and stolen her identity to get a place on the ship. It's only now that she discovers her sister was having an affair with a married security officer who is also now on board The Resolute, looking into suspected falsified records...

LEGENDARY

Joshua Grode
Chief Executive Officer

Mary Parent
Vice Chairman of Worldwide Production

Nick Pepper
President Of Legendary Television & Digital Studios

Ronald Hohauser
Chief Financial Officer

Barnaby Legg
SVP, Creative Strategy

Mike Ross
EVP, Business & Legal Affairs

Dan Feinberg
SVP, Corporate Counsel

Bayan Laird
VP, Business & Legal Affairs

Legendary Comics

Robert Napton
SVP, Publishing

Nikita Kannekanti
Editor

Jann Jones
Manager, Brand Development & Publishing Operations

FIRST PRINTING: OCTOBER 2018

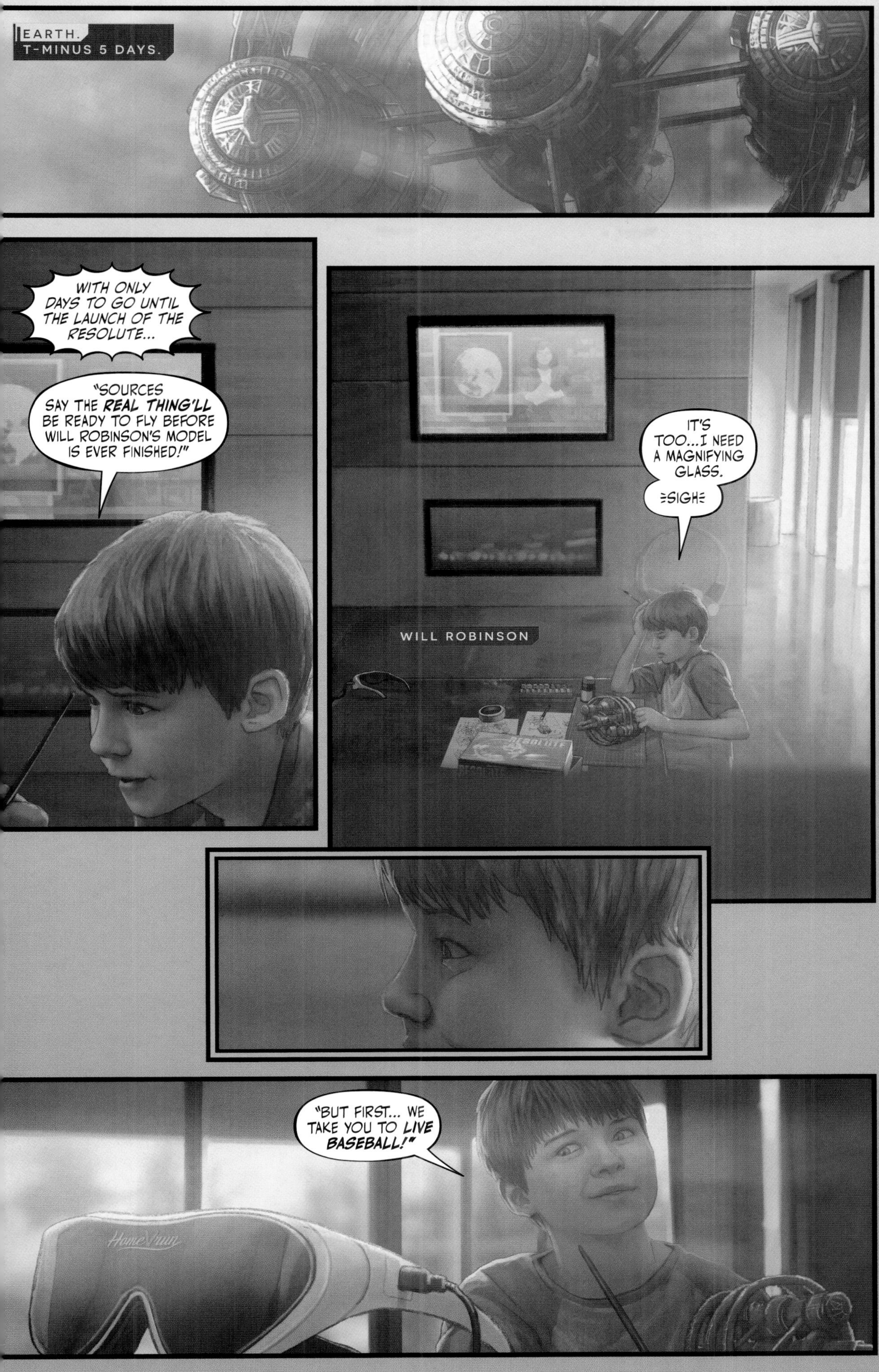
EARTH.
T-MINUS 5 DAYS.
WITH ONLY DAYS TO GO UNTIL THE LAUNCH OF THE RESOLUTE...
"SOURCES SAY THE REAL THING'LL BE READY TO FLY BEFORE WILL ROBINSON'S MODEL IS EVER FINISHED!"
IT'S TOO...I NEED A MAGNIFYING GLASS.
≈SIGH≈
WILL ROBINSON
"BUT FIRST... WE TAKE YOU TO LIVE BASEBALL!"

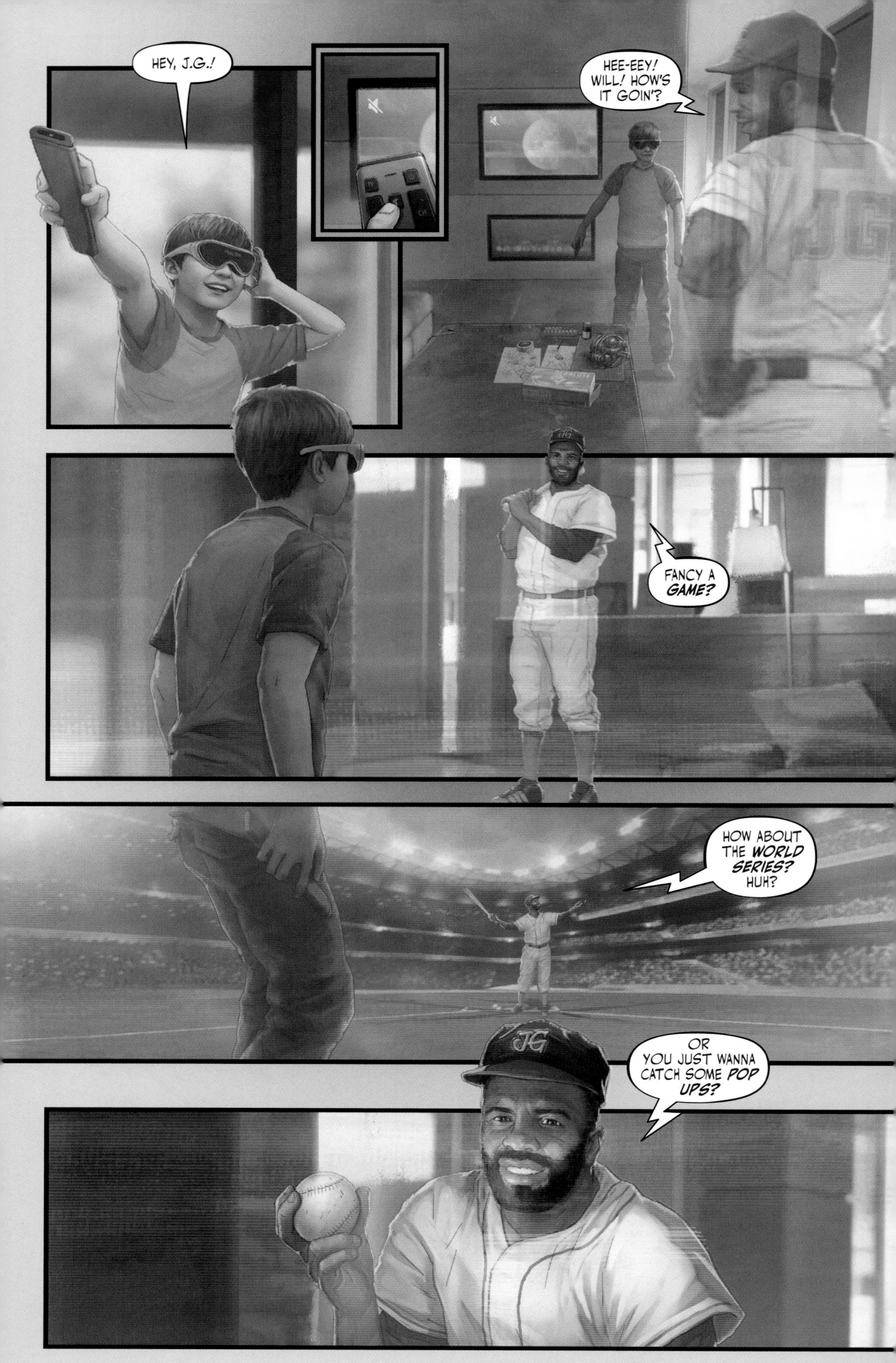
HEY, J.G.!
HEE-EEY! WILL! HOW'S IT GOIN'?
FANCY A GAME?
HOW ABOUT THE WORLD SERIES? HUH?
OR YOU JUST WANNA CATCH SOME POP UPS?

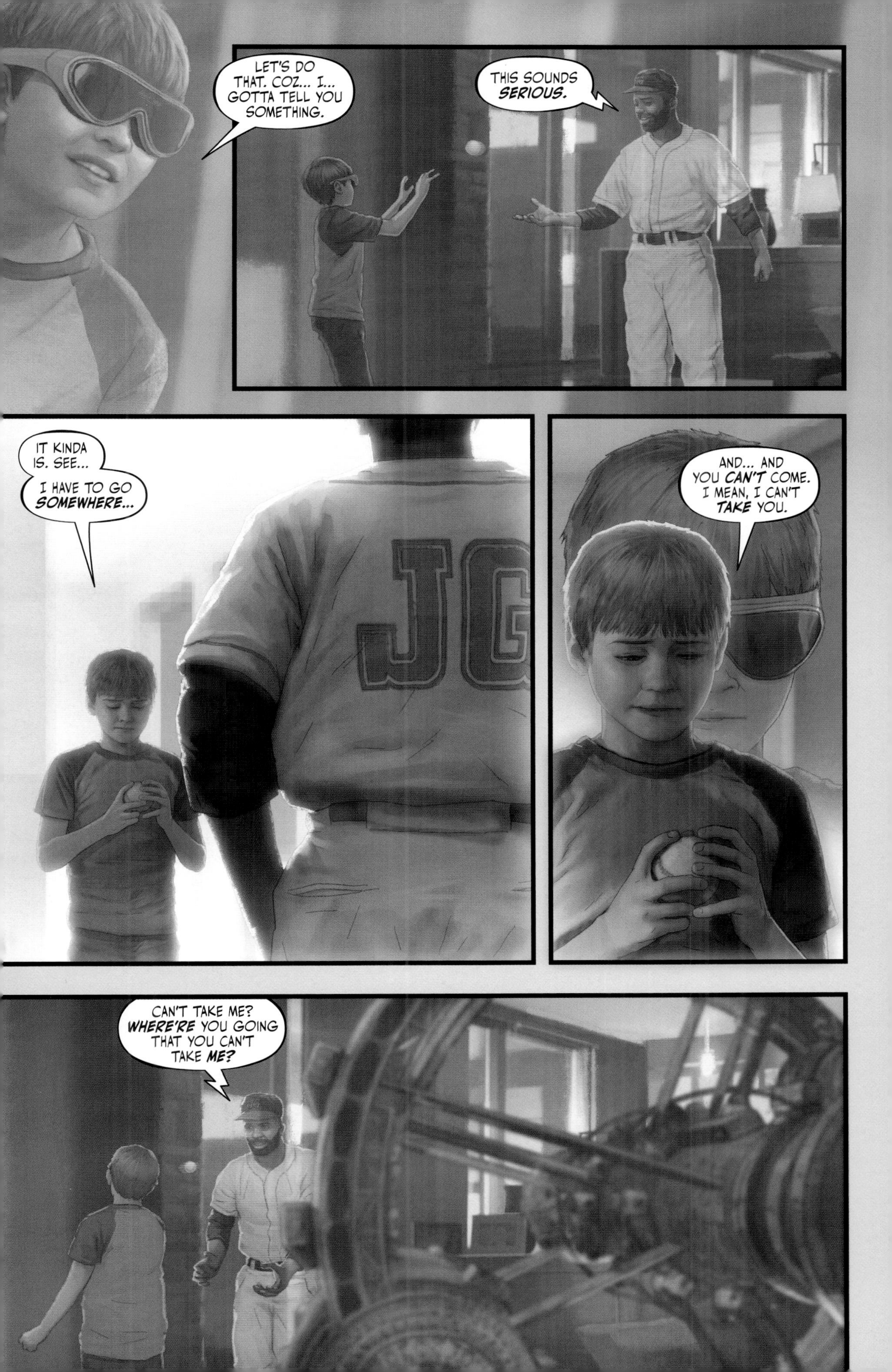

LET'S DO THAT. COZ... I... GOTTA TELL YOU SOMETHING.
THIS SOUNDS *SERIOUS.*
IT KINDA IS. SEE...
I HAVE TO GO *SOMEWHERE...*
JG
AND... AND YOU *CAN'T* COME. I MEAN, I CAN'T *TAKE* YOU.
CAN'T TAKE ME? *WHERE'RE* YOU GOING THAT YOU CAN'T TAKE *ME?*

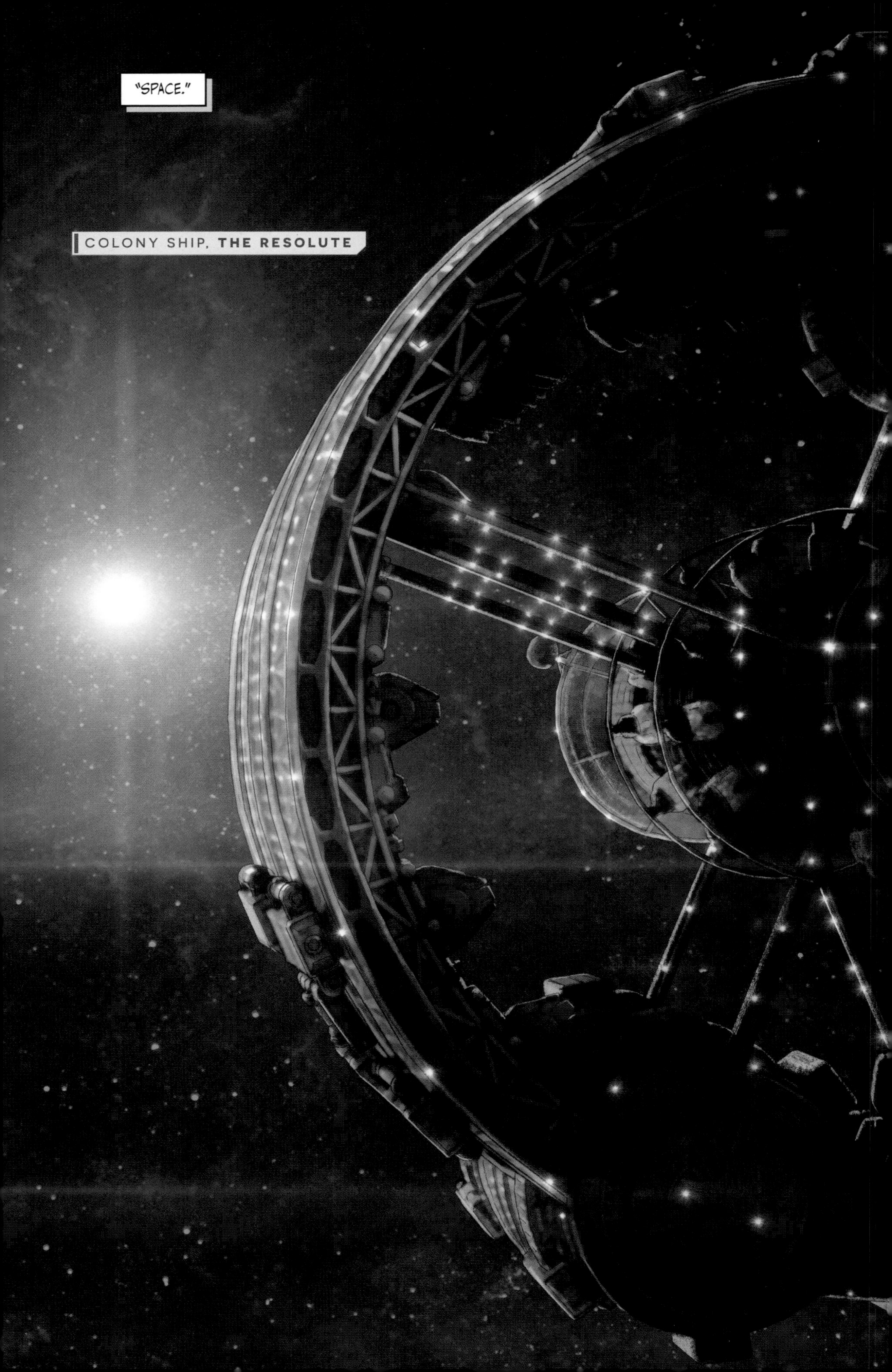
"SPACE."
COLONY SHIP, THE RESOLUTE

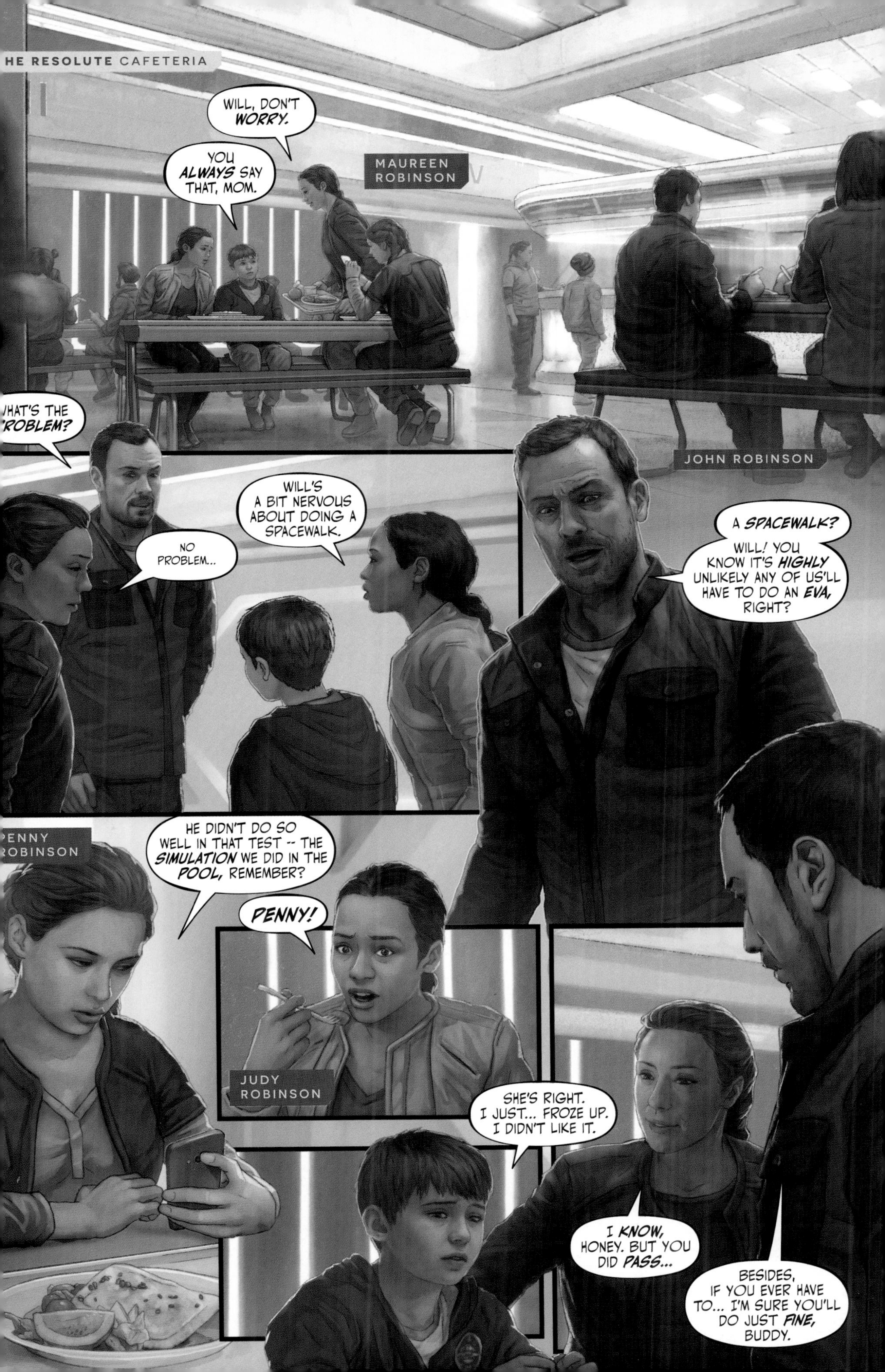
HE RESOLUTE CAFETERIA
WILL, DON'T WORRY.
YOU ALWAYS SAY THAT, MOM.
MAUREEN ROBINSON
WHAT'S THE PROBLEM?
JOHN ROBINSON
NO PROBLEM...
WILL'S A BIT NERVOUS ABOUT DOING A SPACEWALK.
A SPACEWALK?
WILL! YOU KNOW IT'S HIGHLY UNLIKELY ANY OF US'LL HAVE TO DO AN EVA, RIGHT?
PENNY ROBINSON
HE DIDN'T DO SO WELL IN THAT TEST -- THE SIMULATION WE DID IN THE POOL, REMEMBER?
PENNY!
JUDY ROBINSON
SHE'S RIGHT. I JUST... FROZE UP. I DIDN'T LIKE IT.
I KNOW, HONEY. BUT YOU DID PASS...
BESIDES, IF YOU EVER HAVE TO... I'M SURE YOU'LL DO JUST FINE, BUDDY.

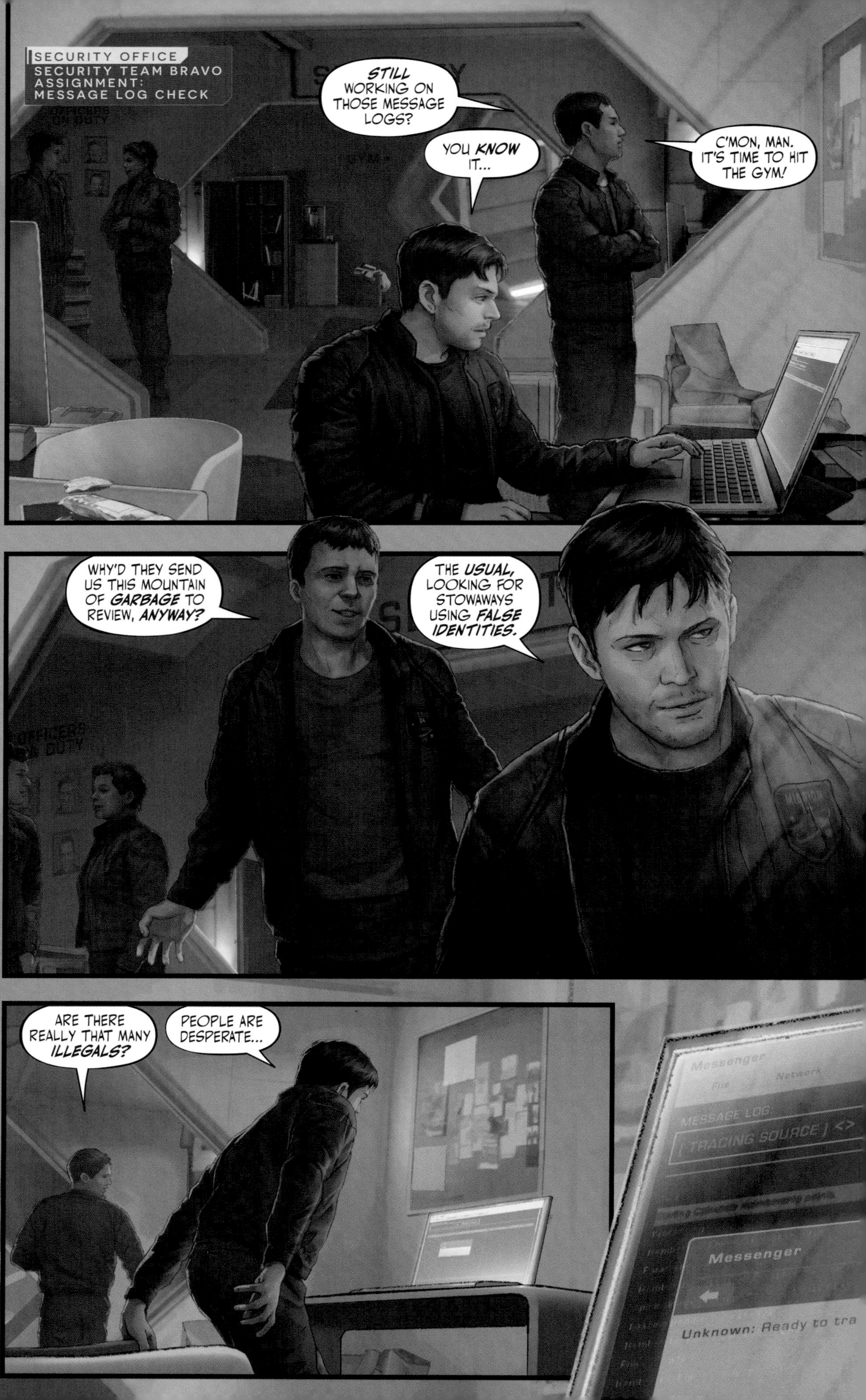
SECURITY OFFICE
SECURITY TEAM BRAVO ASSIGNMENT: MESSAGE LOG CHECK
STILL WORKING ON THOSE MESSAGE LOGS?
YOU KNOW IT...
C'MON, MAN. IT'S TIME TO HIT THE GYM!
WHY'D THEY SEND US THIS MOUNTAIN OF GARBAGE TO REVIEW, ANYWAY?
THE USUAL, LOOKING FOR STOWAWAYS USING FALSE IDENTITIES.
ARE THERE REALLY THAT MANY ILLEGALS?
PEOPLE ARE DESPERATE...
Messenger
File
Network
MESSAGE LOG:
TRACING SOURCE | <>
Messenger
Unknown: Ready to tra

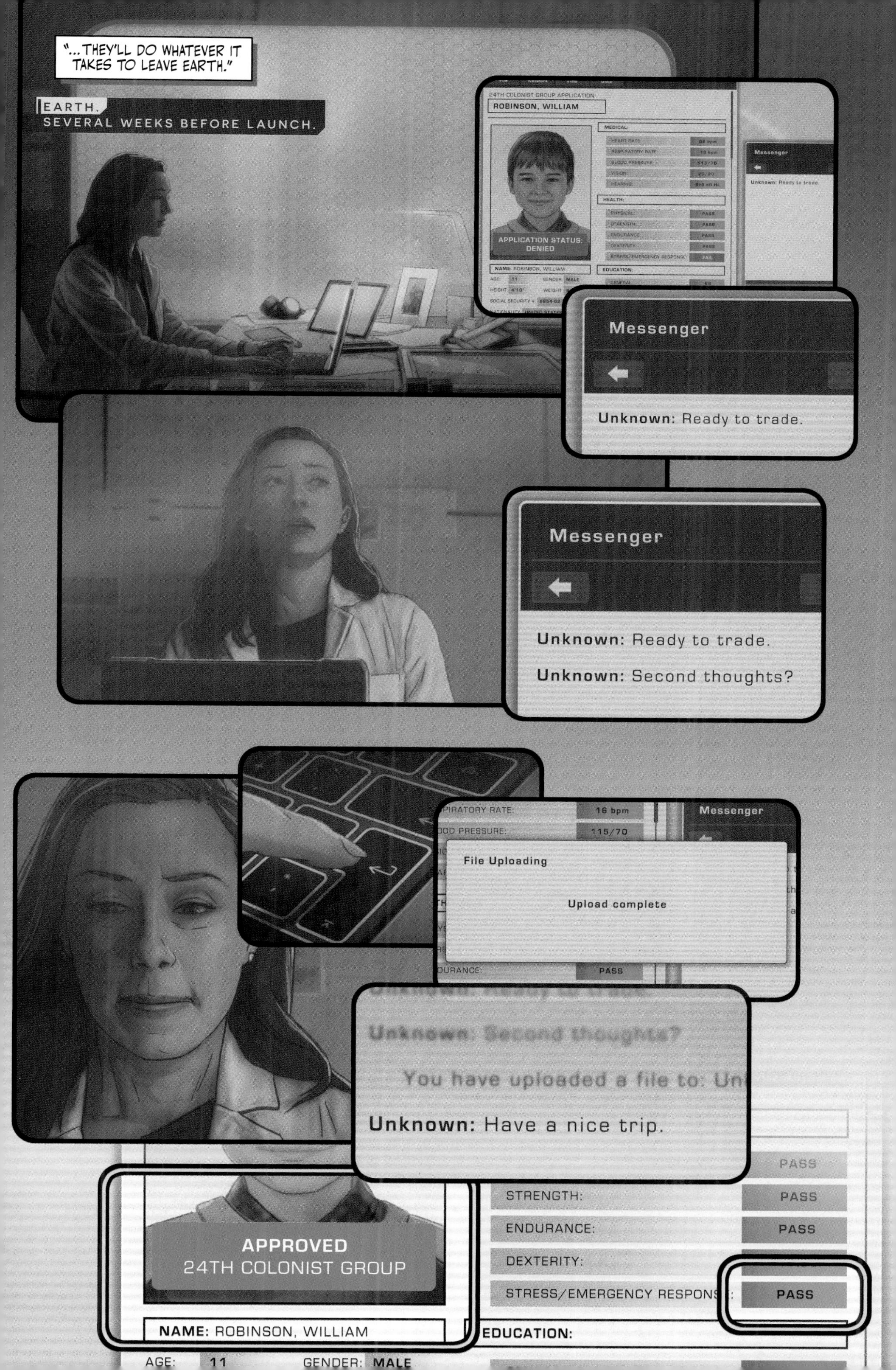

"...THEY'LL DO WHATEVER IT TAKES TO LEAVE EARTH."
EARTH.
SEVERAL WEEKS BEFORE LAUNCH.
24TH COLONIST GROUP APPLICATION:
ROBINSON, WILLIAM
MEDICAL:
HEALTH:
APPLICATION STATUS: DENIED
NAME: ROBINSON, WILLIAM
EDUCATION:
Messenger
Unknown: Ready to trade.
Messenger
Unknown: Ready to trade.
Messenger
Unknown: Ready to trade.
Unknown: Second thoughts?
Messenger
16 bpm
115/70
File Uploading
Upload complete
PASS
Unknown: Second thoughts?
You have uploaded a file to: Un
Unknown: Have a nice trip.
APPROVED
24TH COLONIST GROUP
NAME: ROBINSON, WILLIAM
AGE: 11
GENDER: MALE
PASS
STRENGTH: PASS
ENDURANCE: PASS
DEXTERITY:
STRESS/EMERGENCY RESPONS : PASS
EDUCATION:

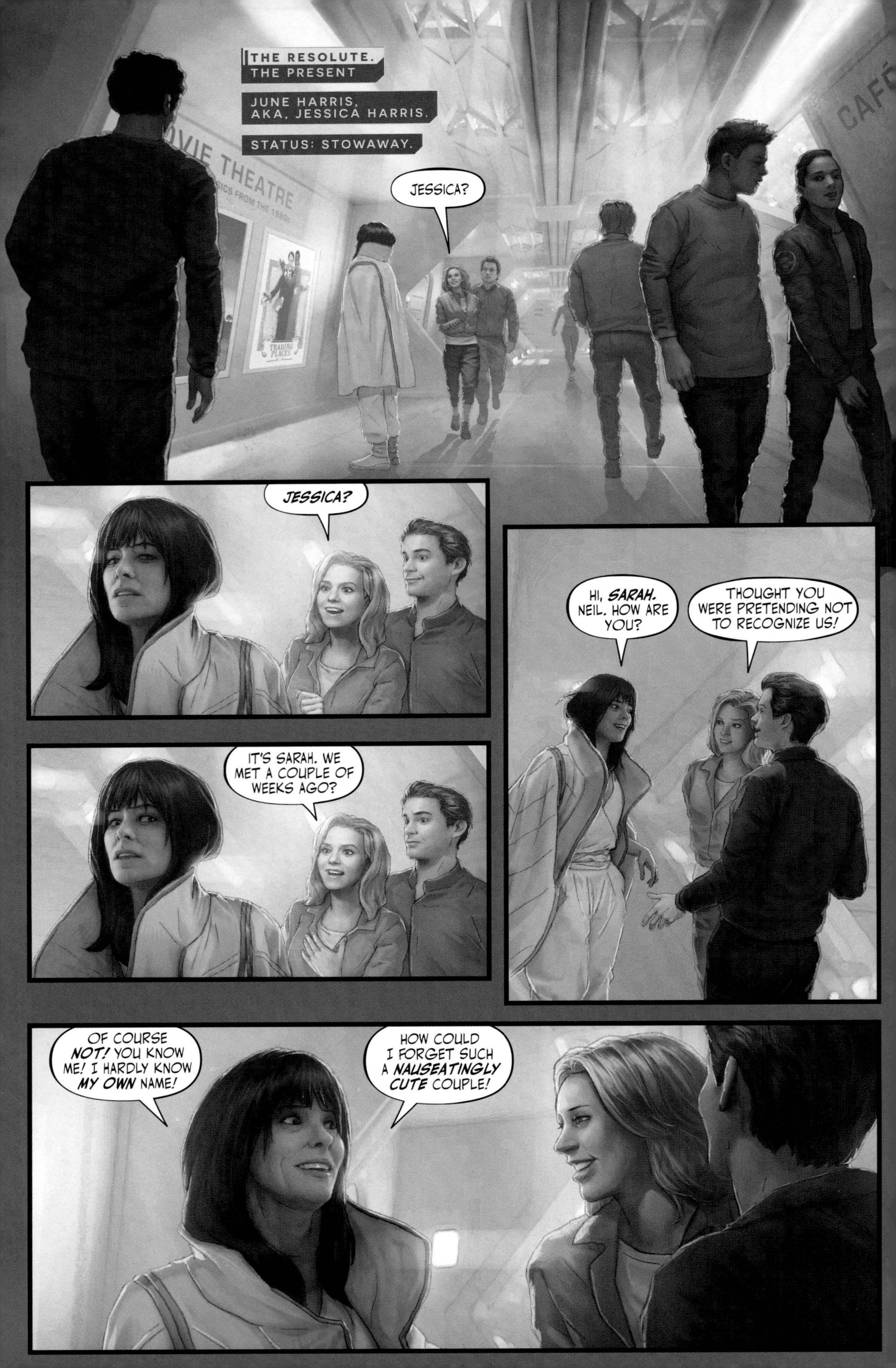
THE RESOLUTE.
THE PRESENT
JUNE HARRIS,
AKA, JESSICA HARRIS.
STATUS: STOWAWAY.
TRADING PLACES
JESSICA?
JESSICA?
IT'S SARAH. WE MET A COUPLE OF WEEKS AGO?
HI, SARAH. NEIL. HOW ARE YOU?
THOUGHT YOU WERE PRETENDING NOT TO RECOGNIZE US!
OF COURSE NOT! YOU KNOW ME! I HARDLY KNOW MY OWN NAME!
HOW COULD I FORGET SUCH A NAUSEATINGLY CUTE COUPLE!

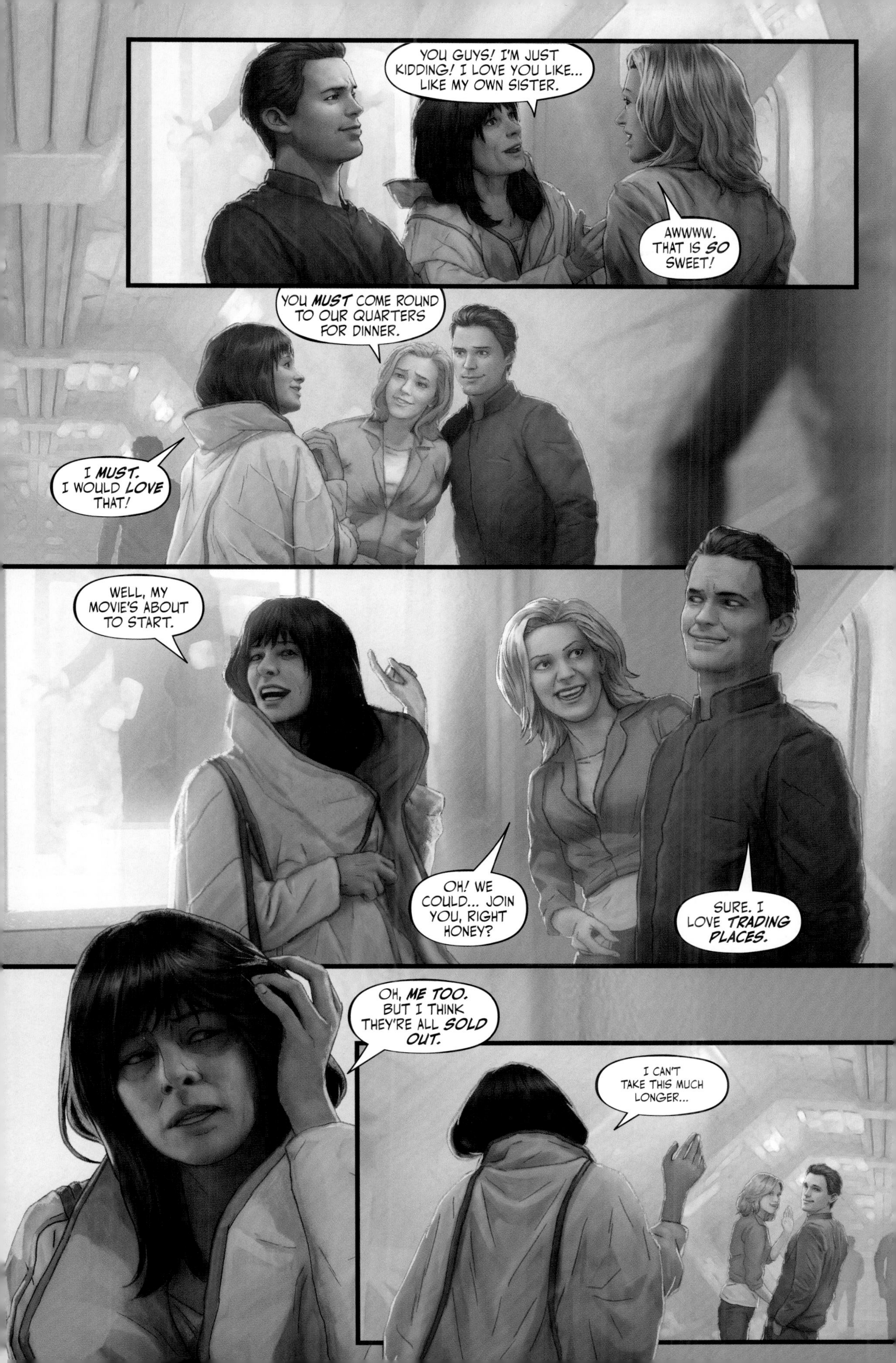
YOU GUYS! I'M JUST KIDDING! I LOVE YOU LIKE... LIKE MY OWN SISTER.
AWWWW. THAT IS *SO* SWEET!
YOU **MUST** COME ROUND TO OUR QUARTERS FOR DINNER.
I **MUST.** I WOULD **LOVE** THAT!
WELL, MY MOVIE'S ABOUT TO START.
OH! WE COULD... JOIN YOU, RIGHT HONEY?
SURE. I LOVE ***TRADING PLACES.***
OH, ***ME TOO.*** BUT I THINK THEY'RE ALL ***SOLD OUT.***
I CAN'T TAKE THIS MUCH LONGER...

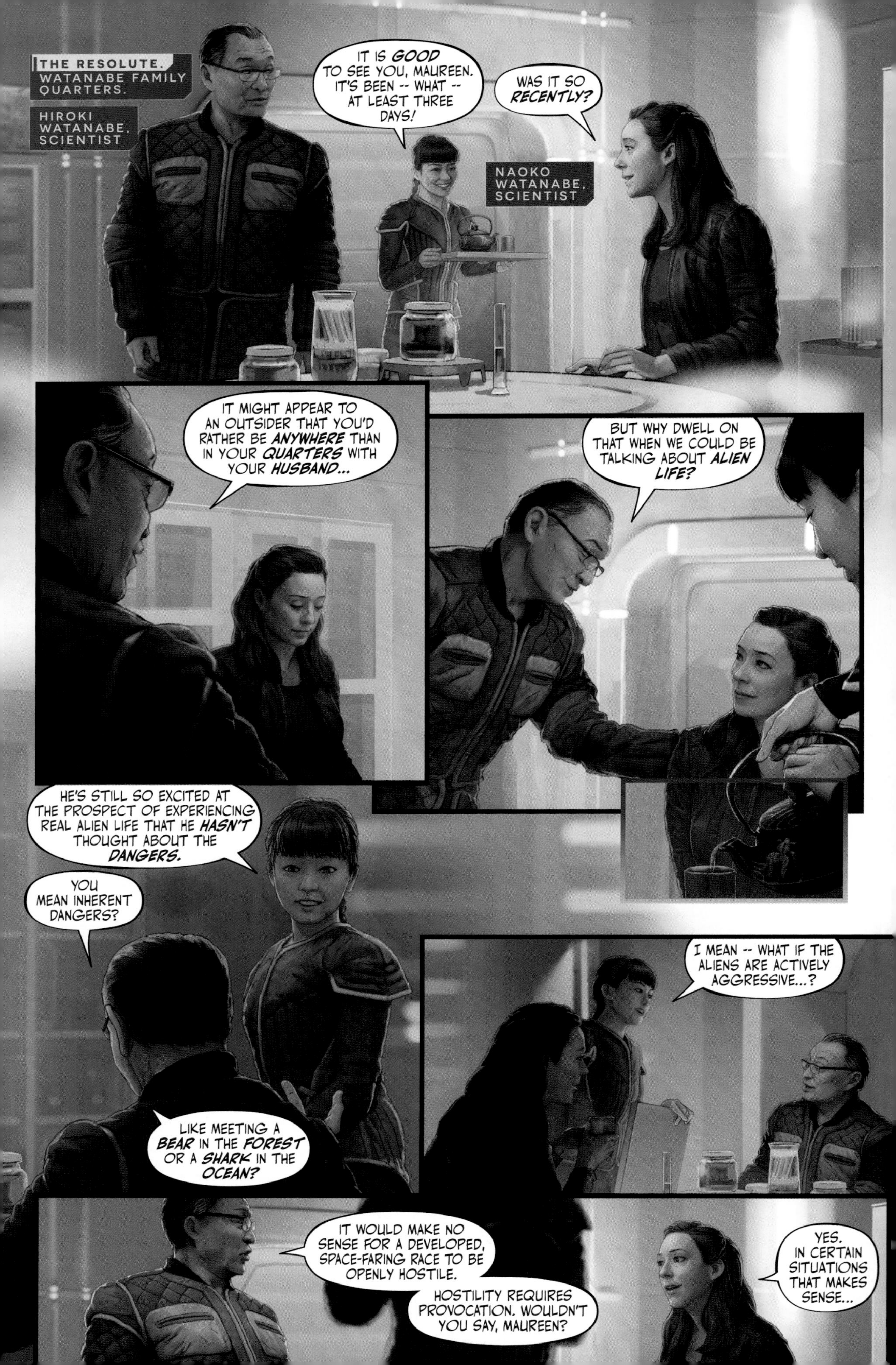
THE RESOLUTE. WATANABE FAMILY QUARTERS.
HIROKI WATANABE, SCIENTIST
IT IS GOOD TO SEE YOU, MAUREEN. IT'S BEEN -- WHAT -- AT LEAST THREE DAYS!
WAS IT SO RECENTLY?
NAOKO WATANABE, SCIENTIST
IT MIGHT APPEAR TO AN OUTSIDER THAT YOU'D RATHER BE ANYWHERE THAN IN YOUR QUARTERS WITH YOUR HUSBAND...
BUT WHY DWELL ON THAT WHEN WE COULD BE TALKING ABOUT ALIEN LIFE?
HE'S STILL SO EXCITED AT THE PROSPECT OF EXPERIENCING REAL ALIEN LIFE THAT HE HASN'T THOUGHT ABOUT THE DANGERS.
YOU MEAN INHERENT DANGERS?
LIKE MEETING A BEAR IN THE FOREST OR A SHARK IN THE OCEAN?
I MEAN -- WHAT IF THE ALIENS ARE ACTIVELY AGGRESSIVE...?
IT WOULD MAKE NO SENSE FOR A DEVELOPED, SPACE-FARING RACE TO BE OPENLY HOSTILE.
HOSTILITY REQUIRES PROVOCATION. WOULDN'T YOU SAY, MAUREEN?
YES. IN CERTAIN SITUATIONS THAT MAKES SENSE...

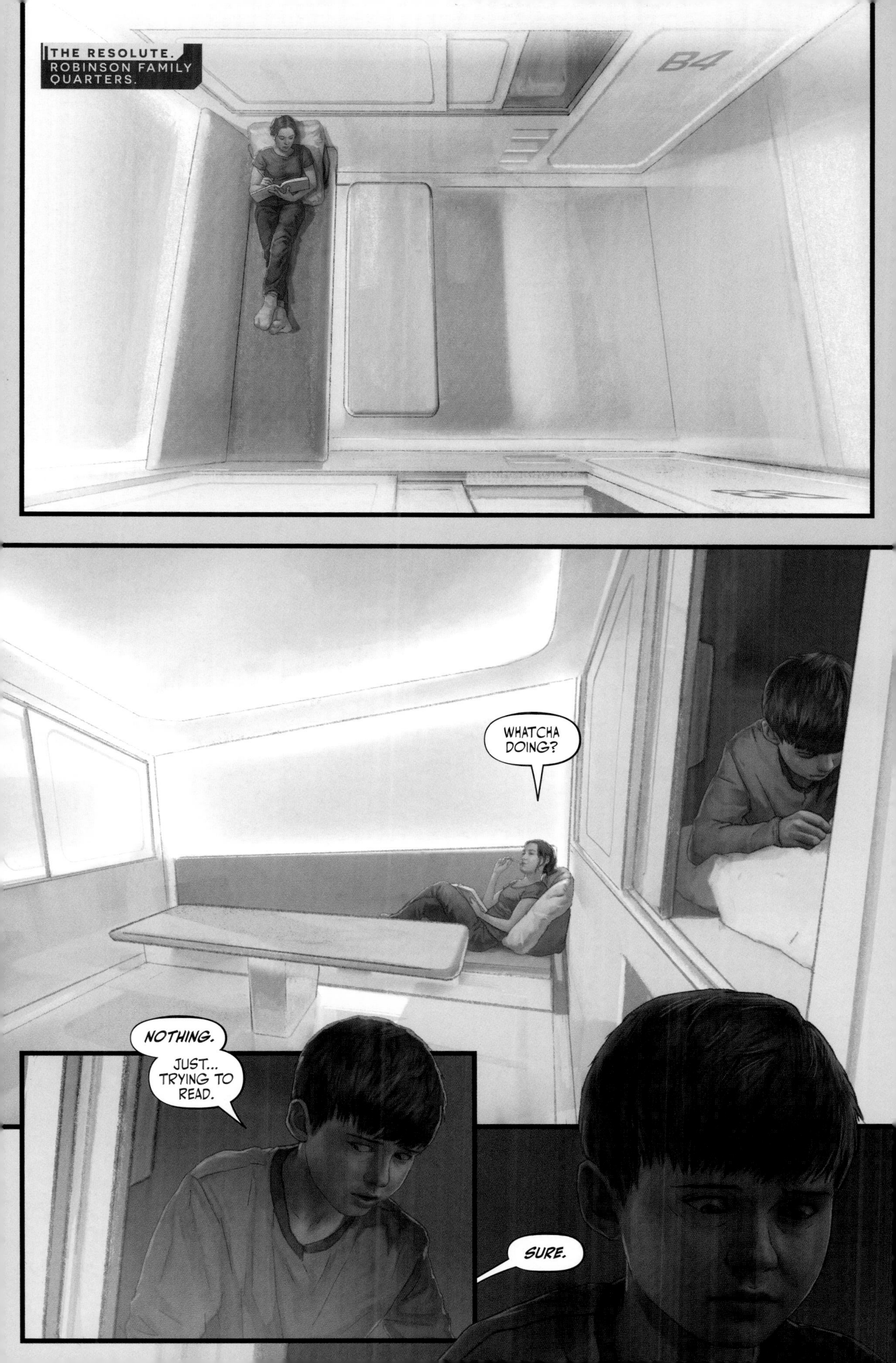
THE RESOLUTE.
ROBINSON FAMILY QUARTERS.
B4
WHATCHA DOING?
NOTHING.
JUST... TRYING TO READ.
SURE.

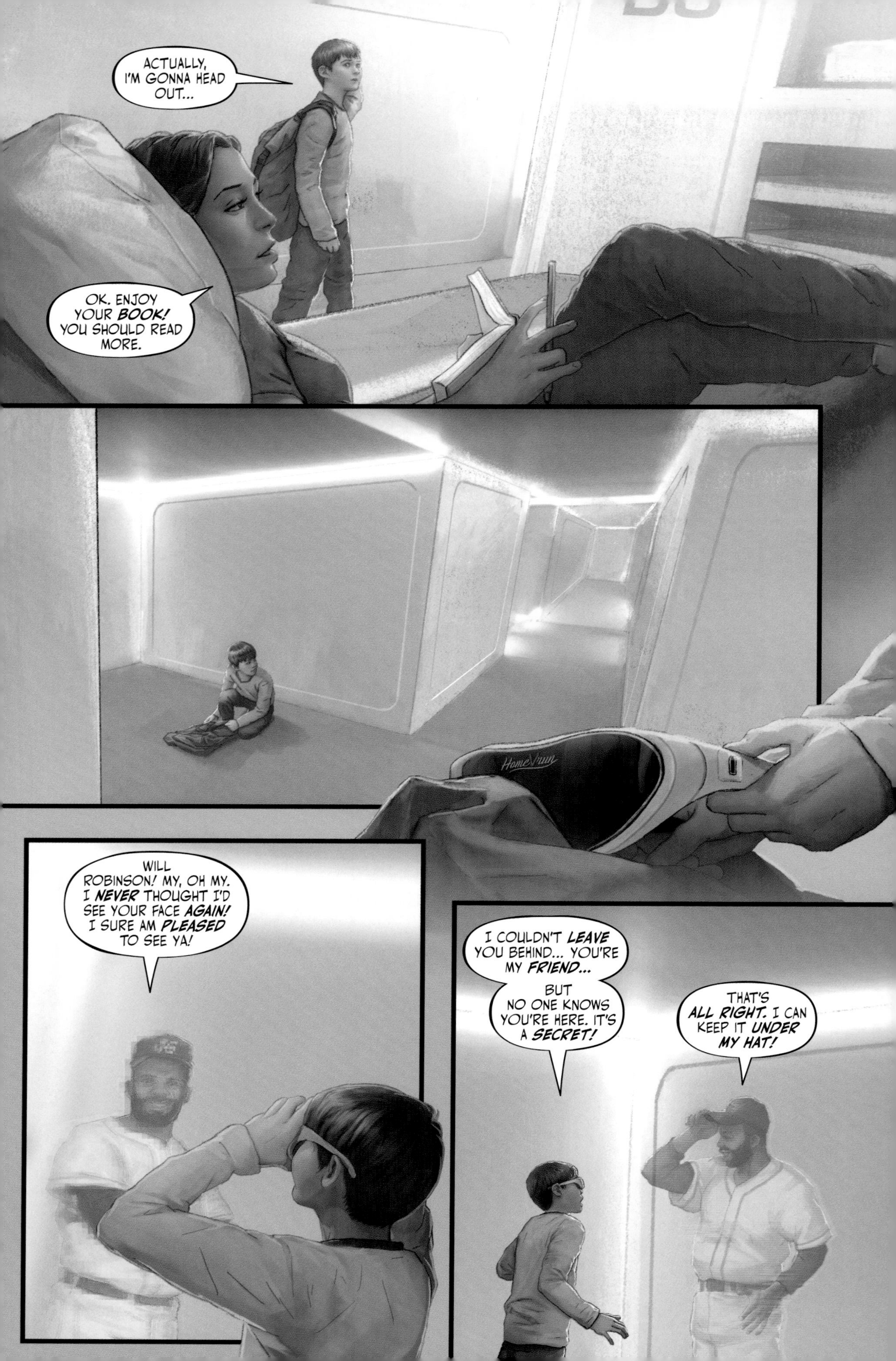
ACTUALLY, I'M GONNA HEAD OUT...
OK. ENJOY YOUR BOOK! YOU SHOULD READ MORE.
WILL ROBINSON! MY, OH MY. I NEVER THOUGHT I'D SEE YOUR FACE AGAIN! I SURE AM PLEASED TO SEE YA!
I COULDN'T LEAVE YOU BEHIND... YOU'RE MY FRIEND...
BUT NO ONE KNOWS YOU'RE HERE. IT'S A SECRET!
THAT'S ALL RIGHT. I CAN KEEP IT UNDER MY HAT!

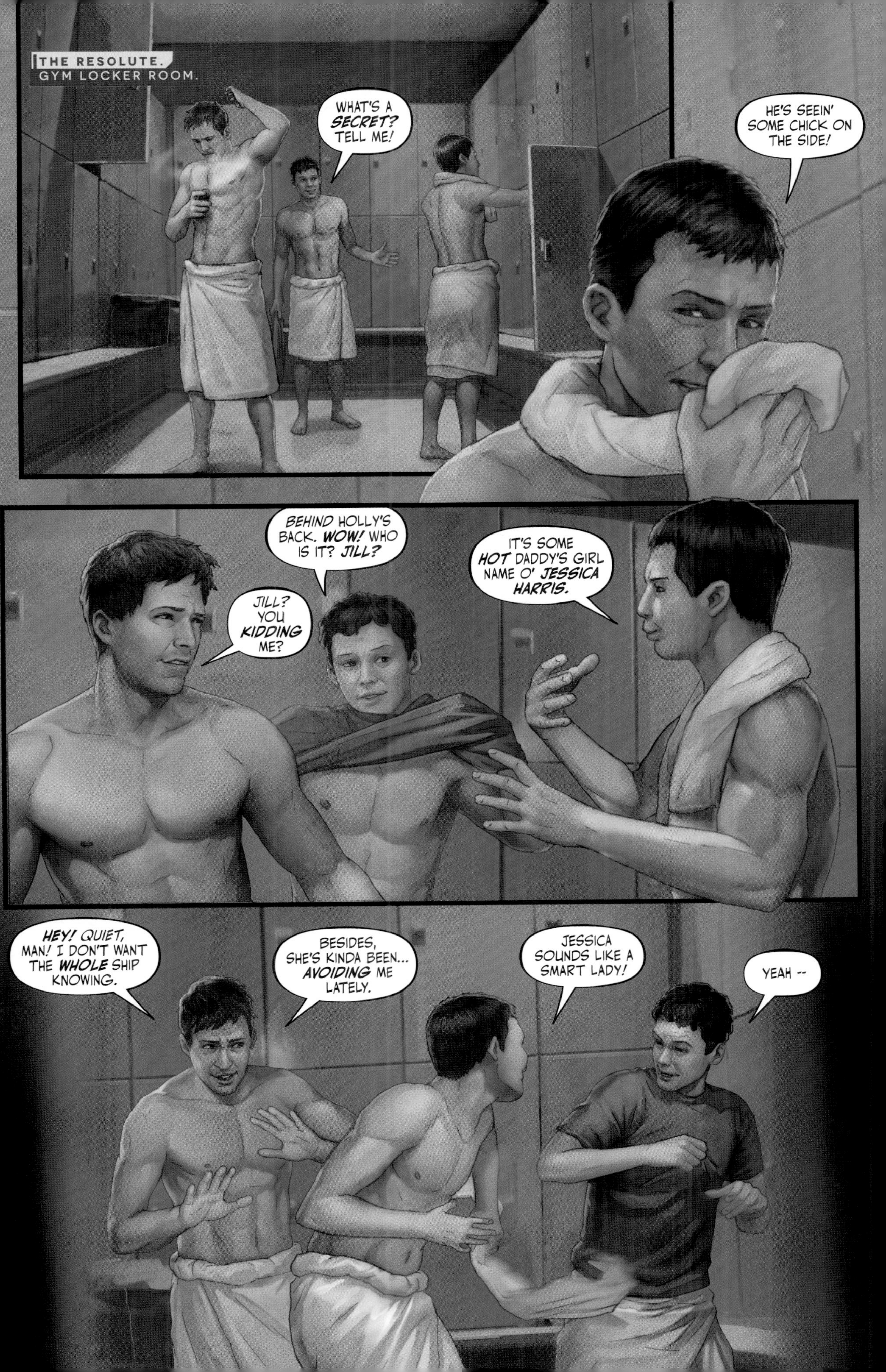
THE RESOLUTE.
GYM LOCKER ROOM.
WHAT'S A SECRET? TELL ME!
HE'S SEEIN' SOME CHICK ON THE SIDE!
BEHIND HOLLY'S BACK. WOW! WHO IS IT? JILL?
JILL? YOU KIDDING ME?
IT'S SOME HOT DADDY'S GIRL NAME O' JESSICA HARRIS.
HEY! QUIET, MAN! I DON'T WANT THE WHOLE SHIP KNOWING.
BESIDES, SHE'S KINDA BEEN... AVOIDING ME LATELY.
JESSICA SOUNDS LIKE A SMART LADY!
YEAH --

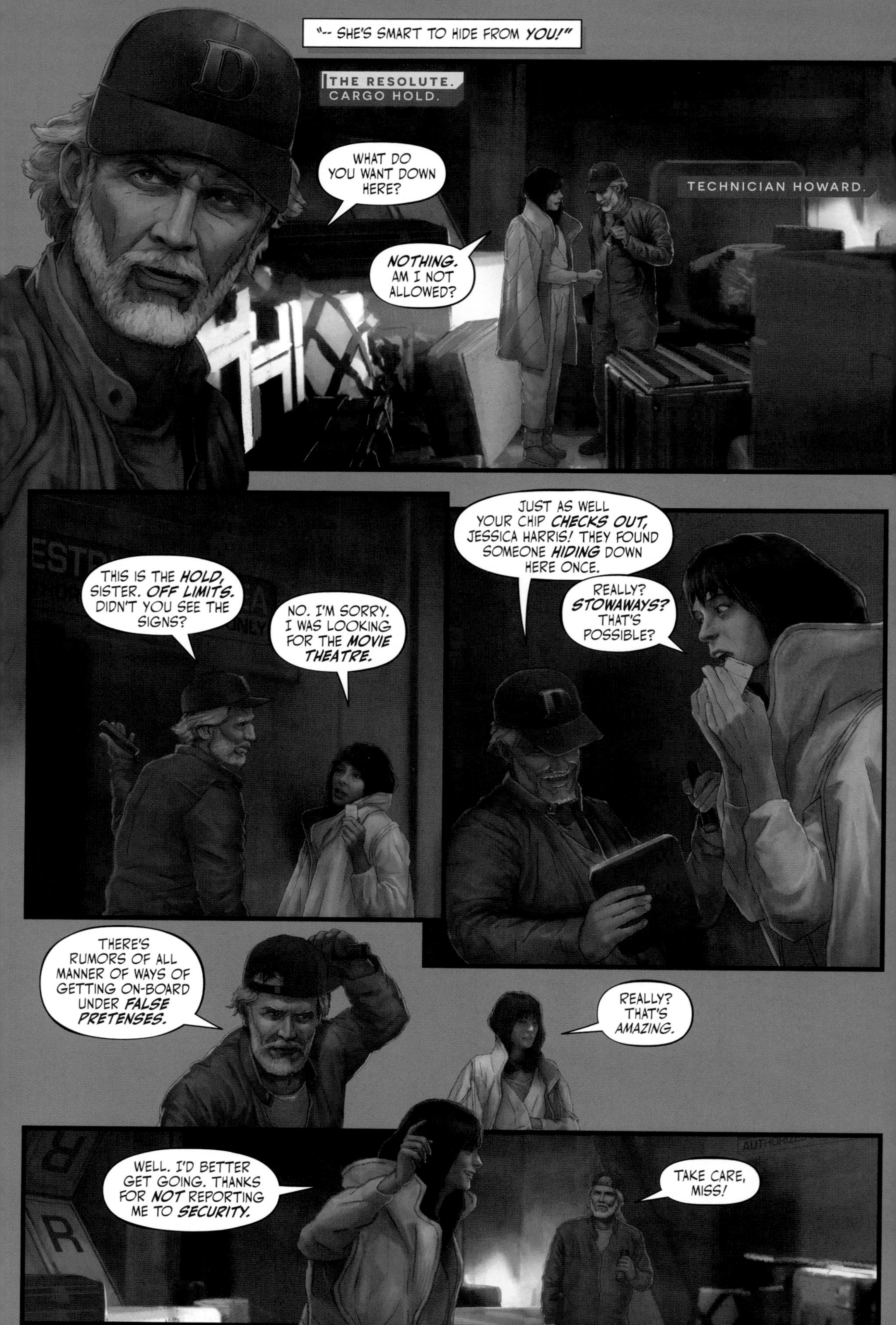
"-- SHE'S SMART TO HIDE FROM YOU!"
THE RESOLUTE. CARGO HOLD.
WHAT DO YOU WANT DOWN HERE?
TECHNICIAN HOWARD.
NOTHING. AM I NOT ALLOWED?
THIS IS THE HOLD, SISTER. OFF LIMITS. DIDN'T YOU SEE THE SIGNS?
NO. I'M SORRY. I WAS LOOKING FOR THE MOVIE THEATRE.
JUST AS WELL YOUR CHIP CHECKS OUT, JESSICA HARRIS! THEY FOUND SOMEONE HIDING DOWN HERE ONCE.
REALLY? STOWAWAYS? THAT'S POSSIBLE?
THERE'S RUMORS OF ALL MANNER OF WAYS OF GETTING ON-BOARD UNDER FALSE PRETENSES.
REALLY? THAT'S AMAZING.
WELL. I'D BETTER GET GOING. THANKS FOR NOT REPORTING ME TO SECURITY.
TAKE CARE, MISS!

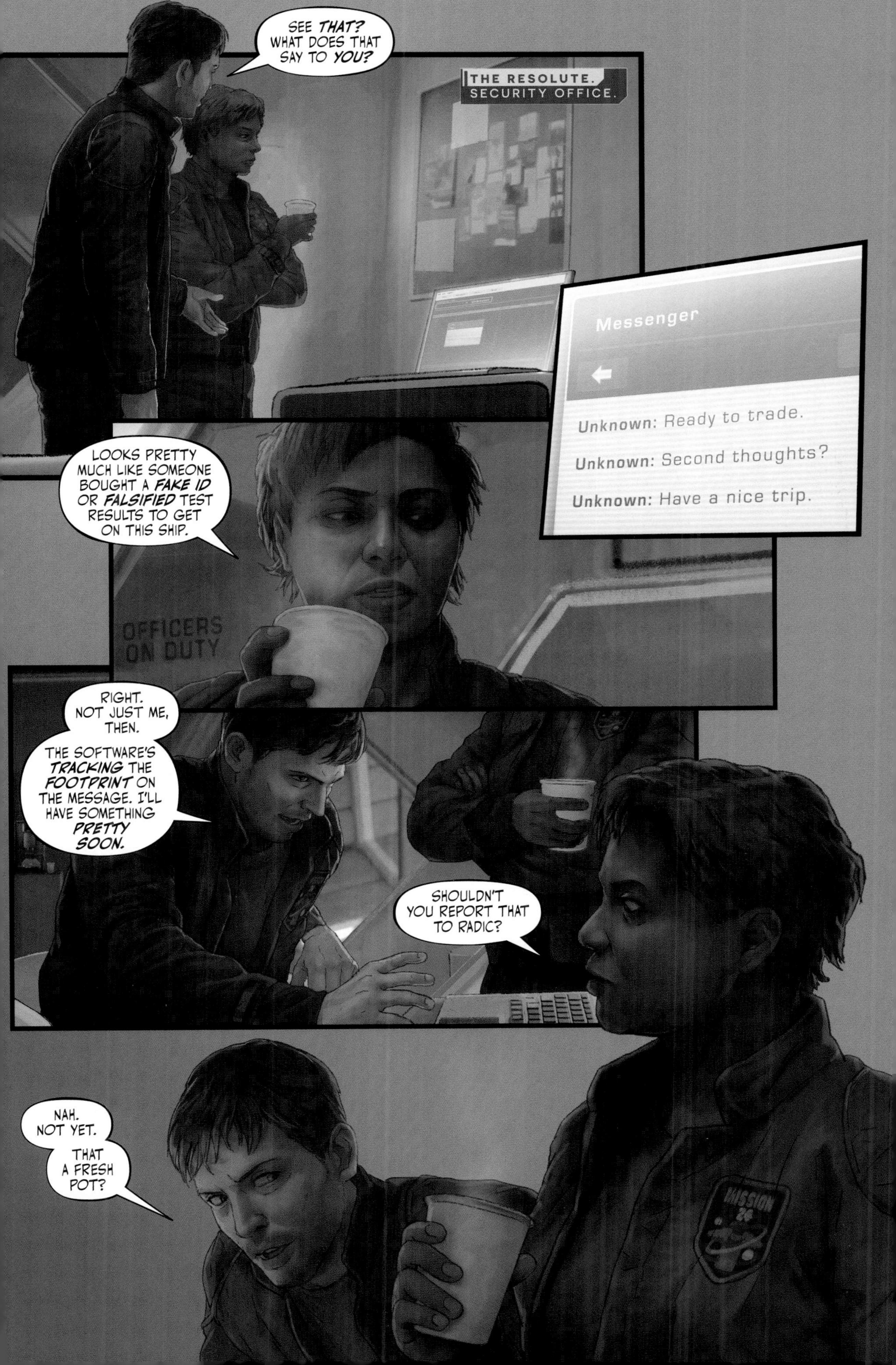

SEE THAT? WHAT DOES THAT SAY TO YOU?
THE RESOLUTE. SECURITY OFFICE.
Messenger
Unknown: Ready to trade.
Unknown: Second thoughts?
Unknown: Have a nice trip.
LOOKS PRETTY MUCH LIKE SOMEONE BOUGHT A FAKE ID OR FALSIFIED TEST RESULTS TO GET ON THIS SHIP.
OFFICERS ON DUTY
RIGHT. NOT JUST ME, THEN.
THE SOFTWARE'S TRACKING THE FOOTPRINT ON THE MESSAGE. I'LL HAVE SOMETHING PRETTY SOON.
SHOULDN'T YOU REPORT THAT TO RADIC?
NAH. NOT YET.
THAT A FRESH POT?
MISSION 26

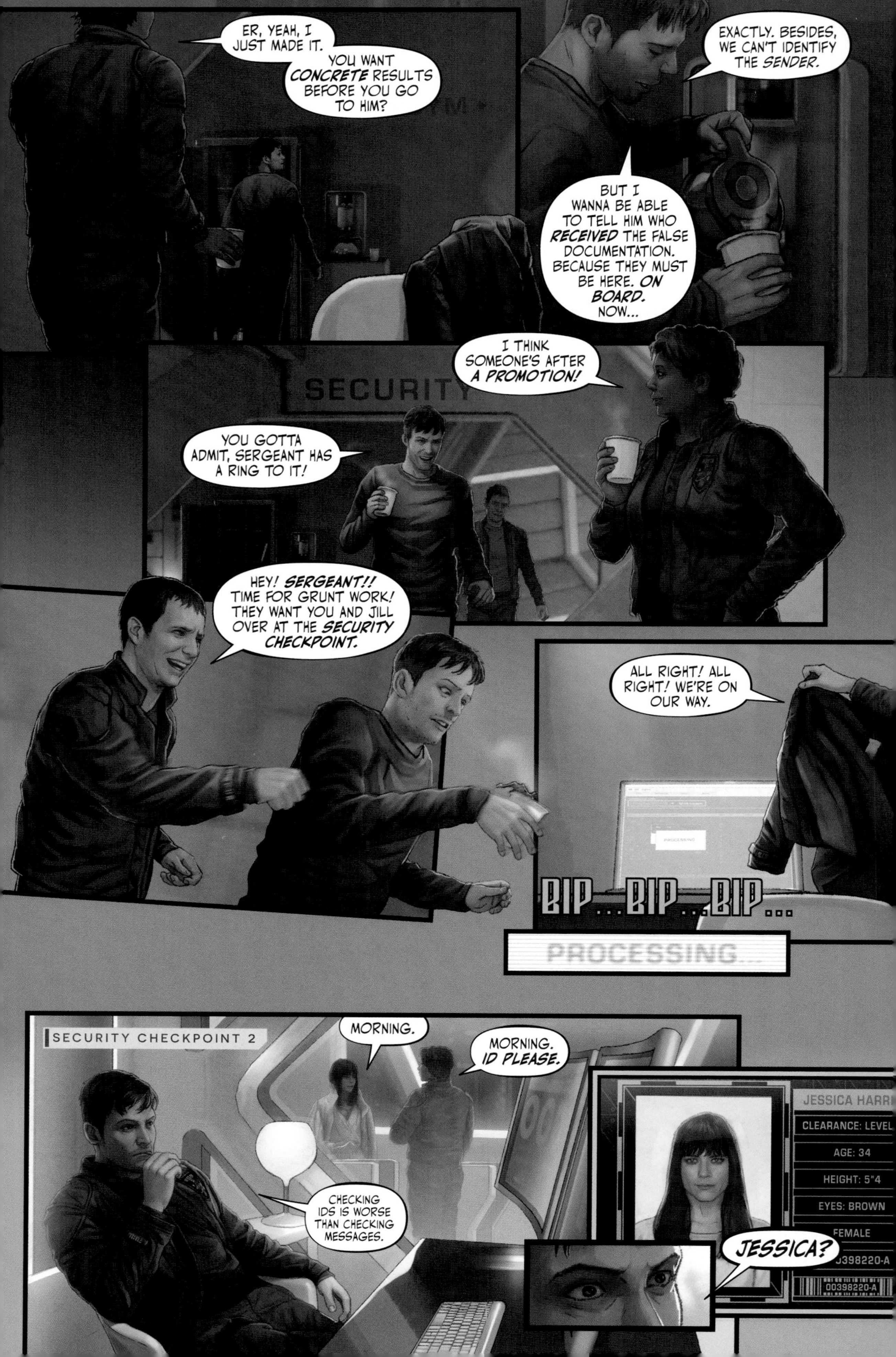
ER, YEAH, I JUST MADE IT.
YOU WANT CONCRETE RESULTS BEFORE YOU GO TO HIM?
EXACTLY. BESIDES, WE CAN'T IDENTIFY THE SENDER.
BUT I WANNA BE ABLE TO TELL HIM WHO RECEIVED THE FALSE DOCUMENTATION. BECAUSE THEY MUST BE HERE. ON BOARD. NOW...
SECURITY
I THINK SOMEONE'S AFTER A PROMOTION!
YOU GOTTA ADMIT, SERGEANT HAS A RING TO IT!
HEY! SERGEANT!! TIME FOR GRUNT WORK! THEY WANT YOU AND JILL OVER AT THE SECURITY CHECKPOINT.
ALL RIGHT! ALL RIGHT! WE'RE ON OUR WAY.
BIP... BIP... BIP...
PROCESSING...
SECURITY CHECKPOINT 2
MORNING.
MORNING. ID PLEASE.
CHECKING IDS IS WORSE THAN CHECKING MESSAGES.
JESSICA HARR
CLEARANCE: LEVEL
AGE: 34
HEIGHT: 5"4
EYES: BROWN
FEMALE
0398220-A
00398220-A
JESSICA?

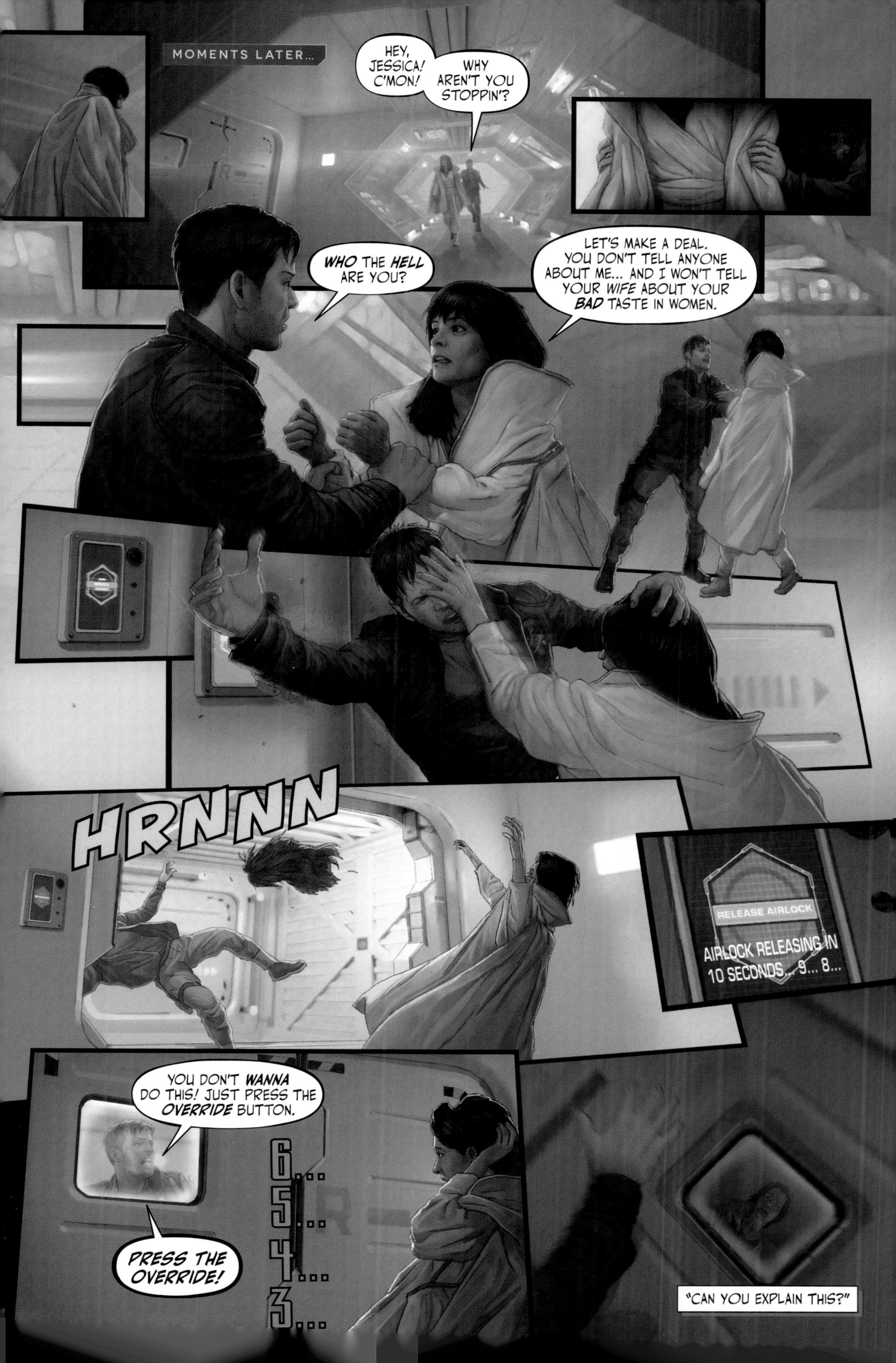
MOMENTS LATER...
HEY, JESSICA! C'MON!
WHY AREN'T YOU STOPPIN'?
WHO THE HELL ARE YOU?
LET'S MAKE A DEAL. YOU DON'T TELL ANYONE ABOUT ME... AND I WON'T TELL YOUR WIFE ABOUT YOUR BAD TASTE IN WOMEN.
HRNNN
RELEASE AIRLOCK
AIRLOCK RELEASING IN 10 SECONDS... 9... 8...
YOU DON'T WANNA DO THIS! JUST PRESS THE OVERRIDE BUTTON.
PRESS THE OVERRIDE!
6...
5...
4...
3...
"CAN YOU EXPLAIN THIS?"

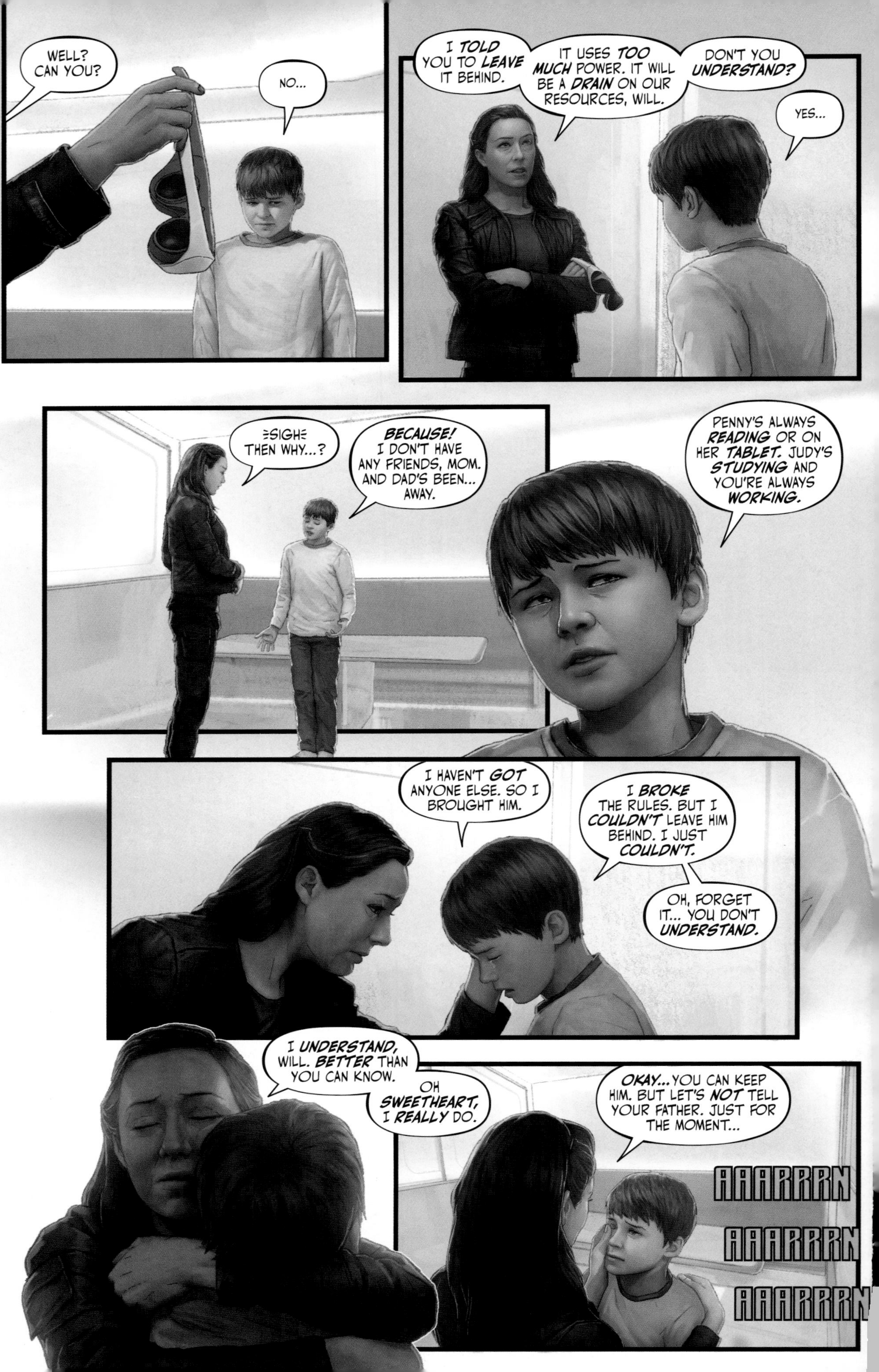
WELL? CAN YOU?
NO...
I TOLD YOU TO LEAVE IT BEHIND.
IT USES TOO MUCH POWER. IT WILL BE A DRAIN ON OUR RESOURCES, WILL.
DON'T YOU UNDERSTAND?
YES...
=SIGH= THEN WHY...?
BECAUSE! I DON'T HAVE ANY FRIENDS, MOM. AND DAD'S BEEN... AWAY.
PENNY'S ALWAYS READING OR ON HER TABLET. JUDY'S STUDYING AND YOU'RE ALWAYS WORKING.
I HAVEN'T GOT ANYONE ELSE. SO I BROUGHT HIM.
I BROKE THE RULES. BUT I COULDN'T LEAVE HIM BEHIND. I JUST COULDN'T.
OH, FORGET IT... YOU DON'T UNDERSTAND.
I UNDERSTAND, WILL. BETTER THAN YOU CAN KNOW.
OH SWEETHEART, I REALLY DO.
OKAY... YOU CAN KEEP HIM. BUT LET'S NOT TELL YOUR FATHER. JUST FOR THE MOMENT...
AAARRRN
AAARRRN
AAARRRN

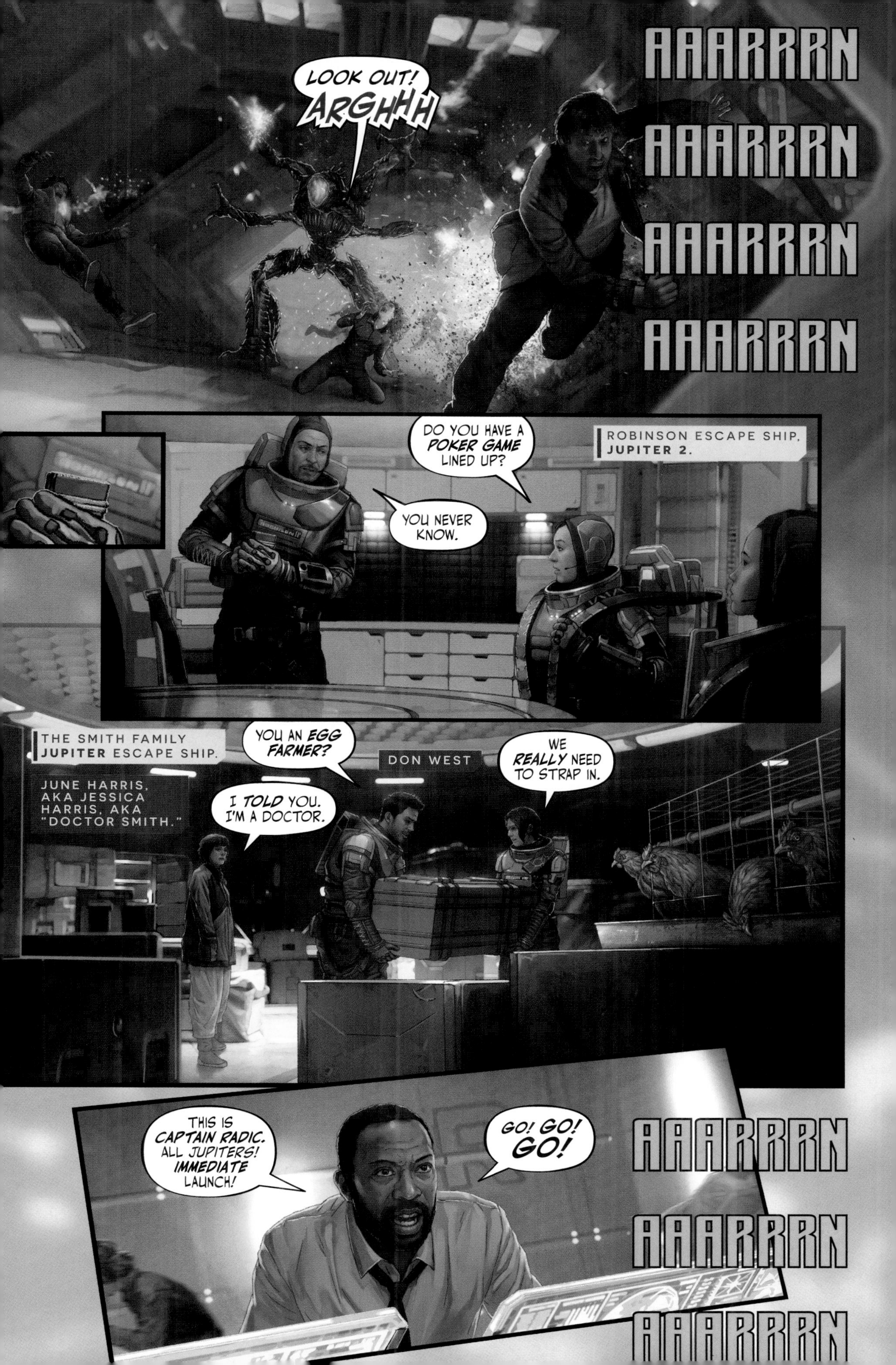
LOOK OUT! ARGHHH
AAARRRN
AAARRRN
AAARRRN
AAARRRN
ROBINSON ESCAPE SHIP, JUPITER 2.
DO YOU HAVE A POKER GAME LINED UP?
YOU NEVER KNOW.
THE SMITH FAMILY JUPITER ESCAPE SHIP.
JUNE HARRIS, AKA JESSICA HARRIS, AKA "DOCTOR SMITH."
YOU AN EGG FARMER?
DON WEST
I TOLD YOU. I'M A DOCTOR.
WE REALLY NEED TO STRAP IN.
THIS IS CAPTAIN RADIC. ALL JUPITERS! IMMEDIATE LAUNCH!
GO! GO! GO!
AAARRRN
AAARRRN
AAARRRN

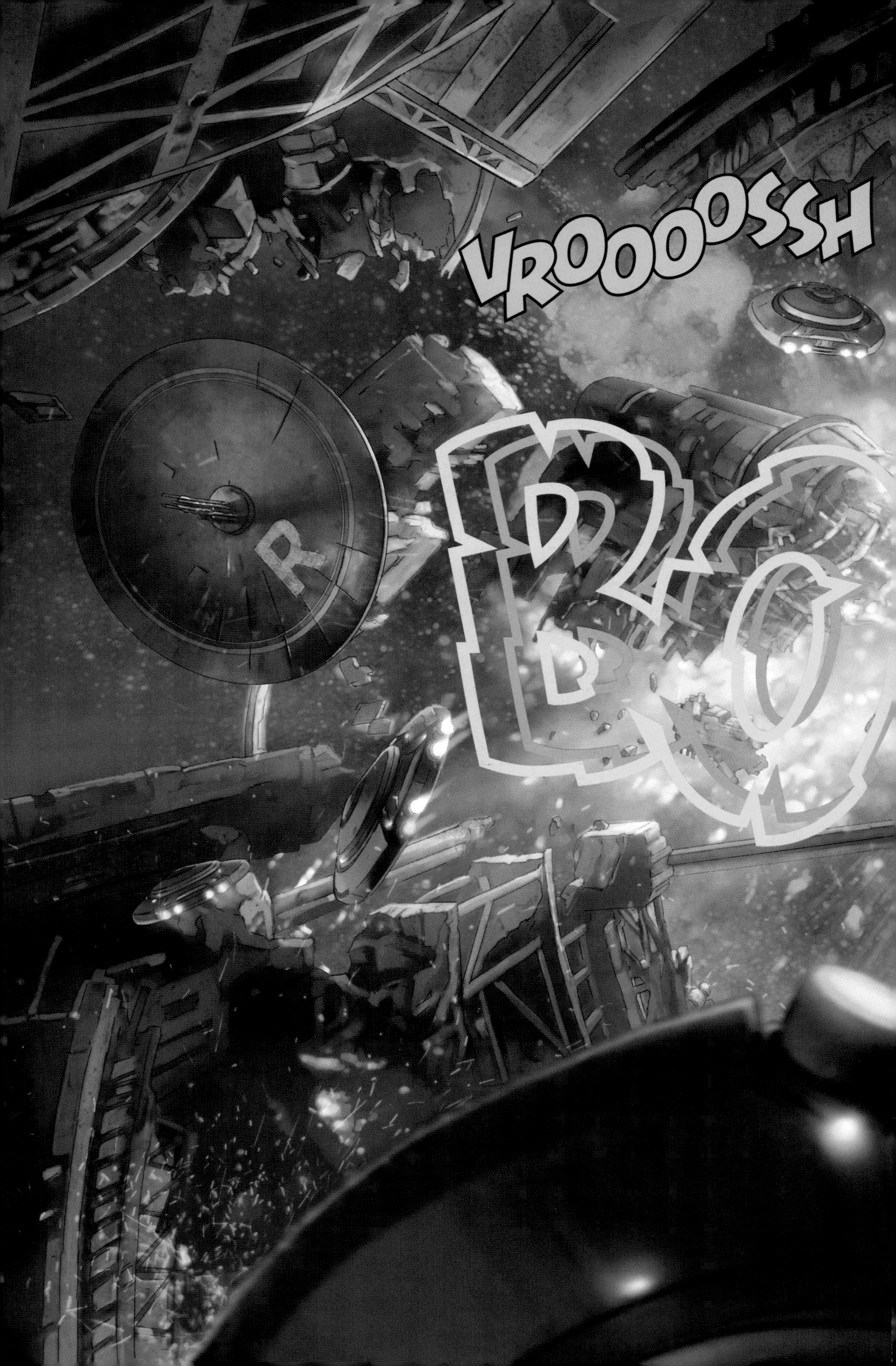
VROOOOSSH

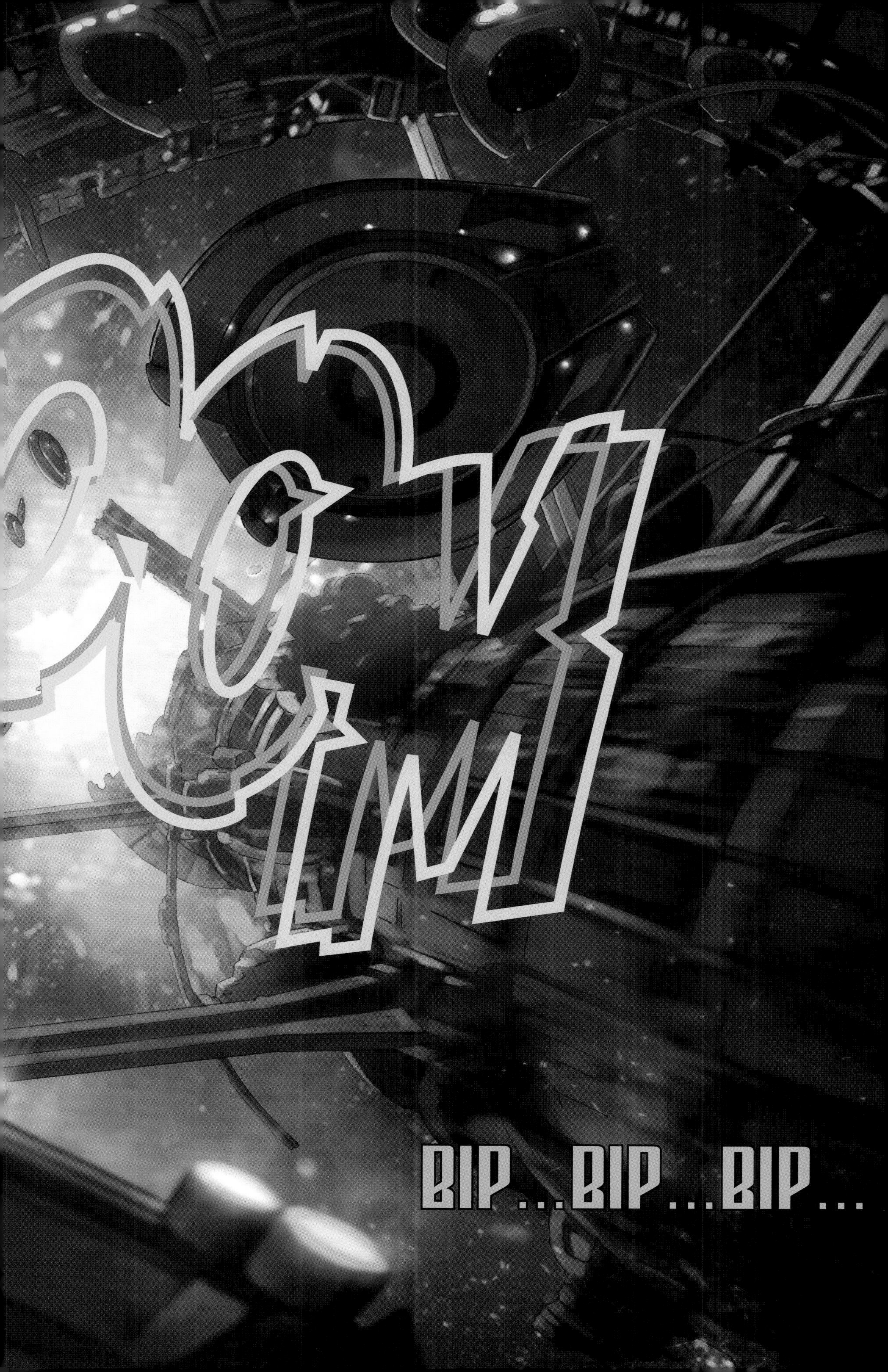
BIP...BIP...BIP...

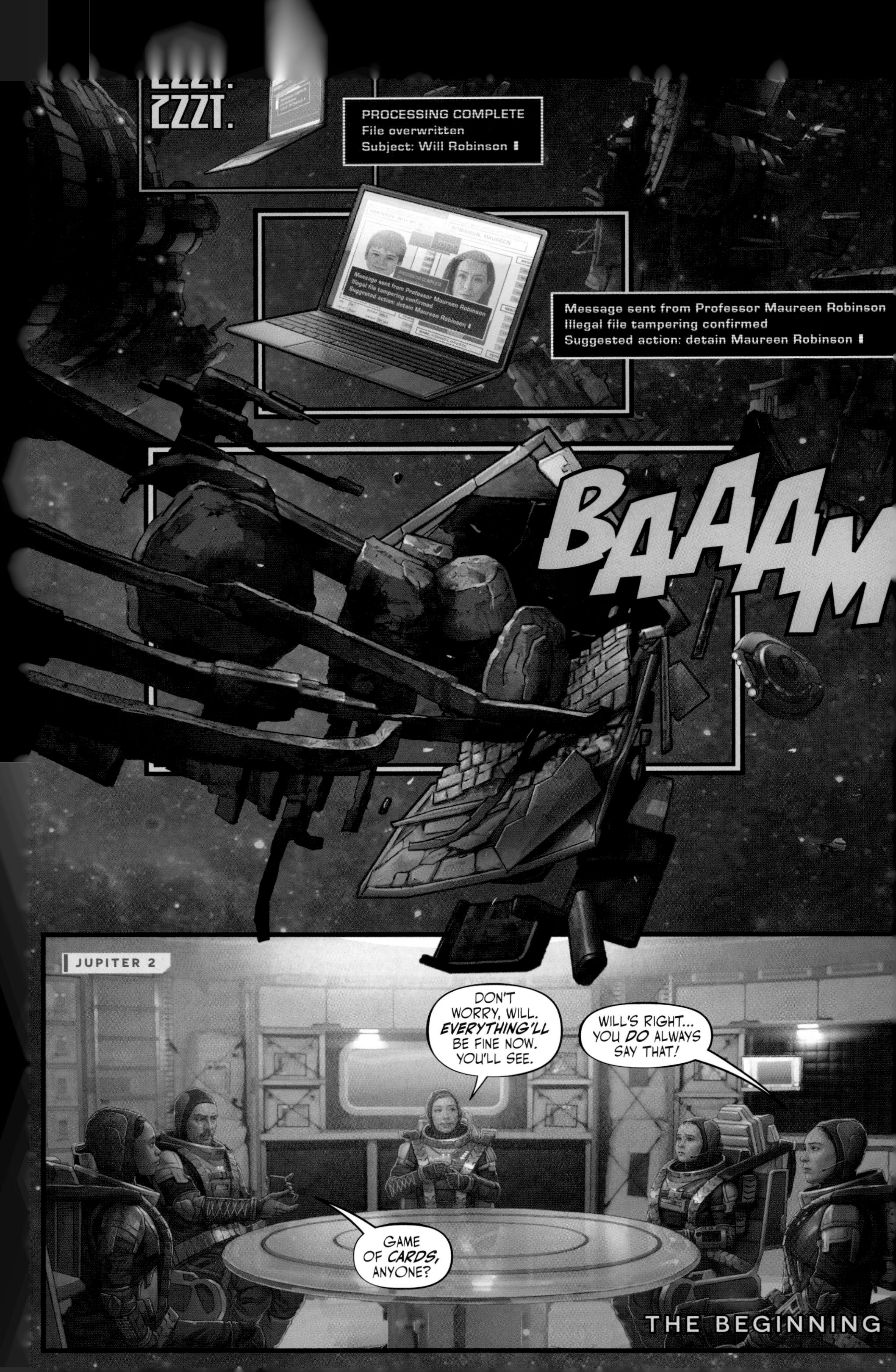
ZZZT.
PROCESSING COMPLETE
File overwritten
Subject: Will Robinson
Message sent from Professor Maureen Robinson
Illegal file tampering confirmed
Suggested action: detain Maureen Robinson
BAAAM
JUPITER 2
DON'T WORRY, WILL. EVERYTHING'LL BE FINE NOW. YOU'LL SEE.
WILL'S RIGHT... YOU DO ALWAYS SAY THAT!
GAME OF CARDS, ANYONE?
THE BEGINNING

"Penny & Judith"

Following their escape from The Resolute after a mysterious attack, the Robinsons crash land the Jupiter 2 in a glacier. They narrowly avoid an avalanche and touch down in a wooded area.

With no fuel left, they have no choice but to begin exploring this alien world...

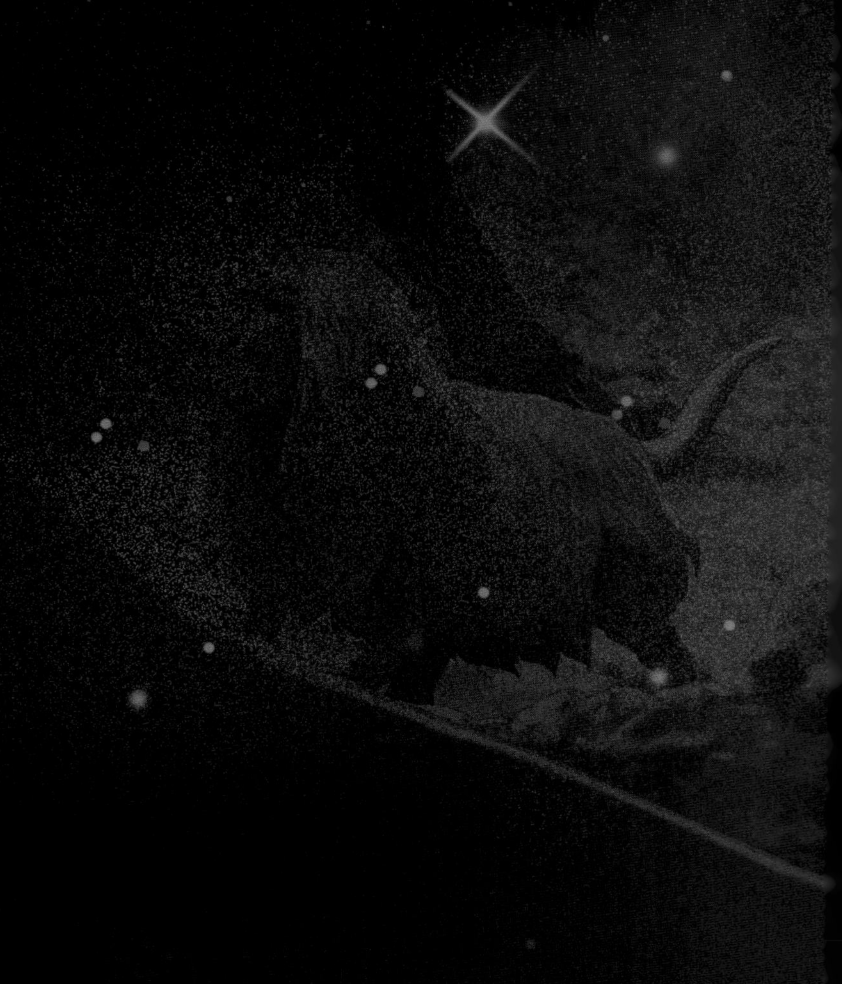

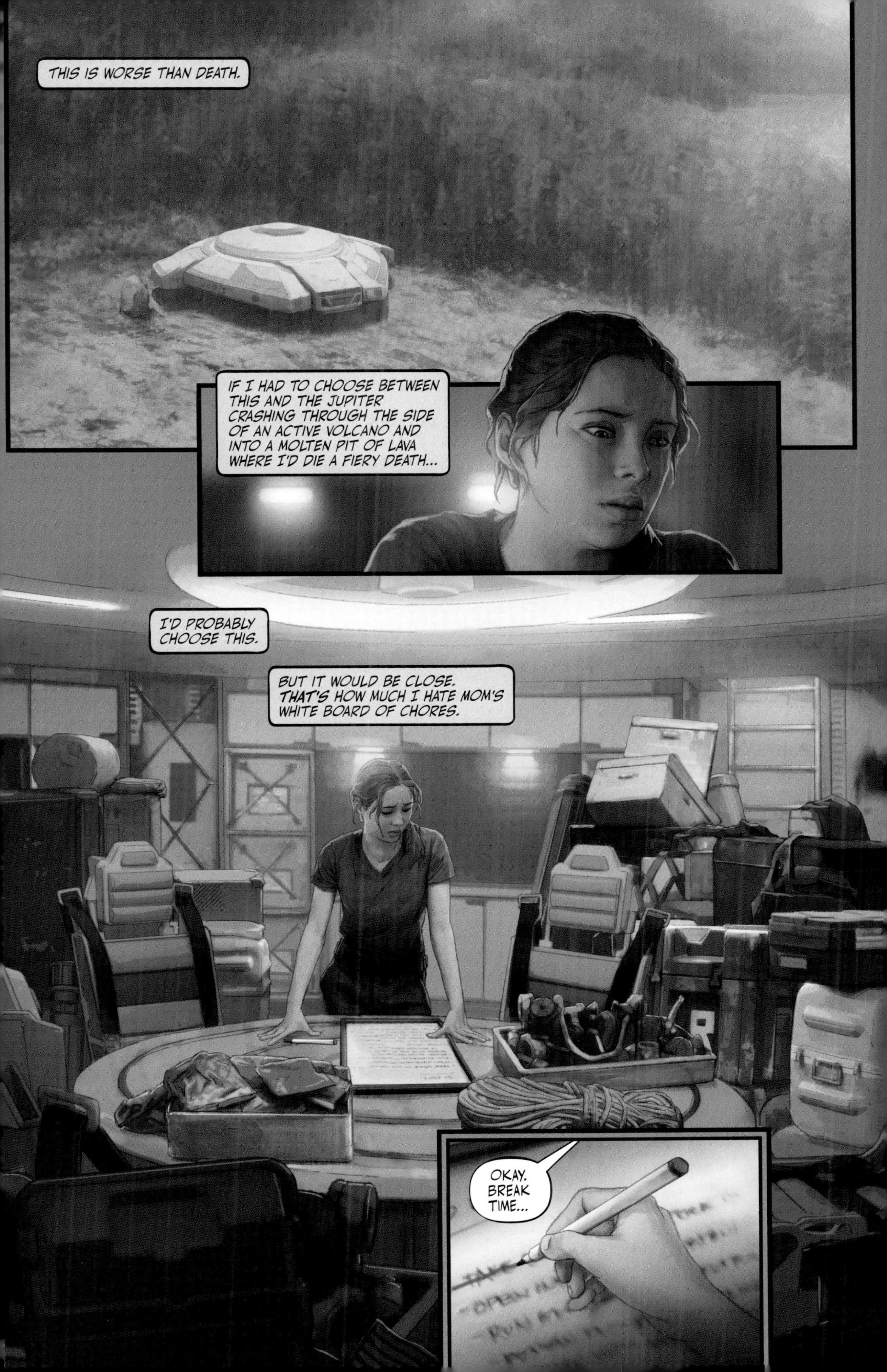
THIS IS WORSE THAN DEATH.
IF I HAD TO CHOOSE BETWEEN THIS AND THE JUPITER CRASHING THROUGH THE SIDE OF AN ACTIVE VOLCANO AND INTO A MOLTEN PIT OF LAVA WHERE I'D DIE A FIERY DEATH...
I'D PROBABLY CHOOSE THIS.
BUT IT WOULD BE CLOSE. THAT'S HOW MUCH I HATE MOM'S WHITE BOARD OF CHORES.
OKAY. BREAK TIME...

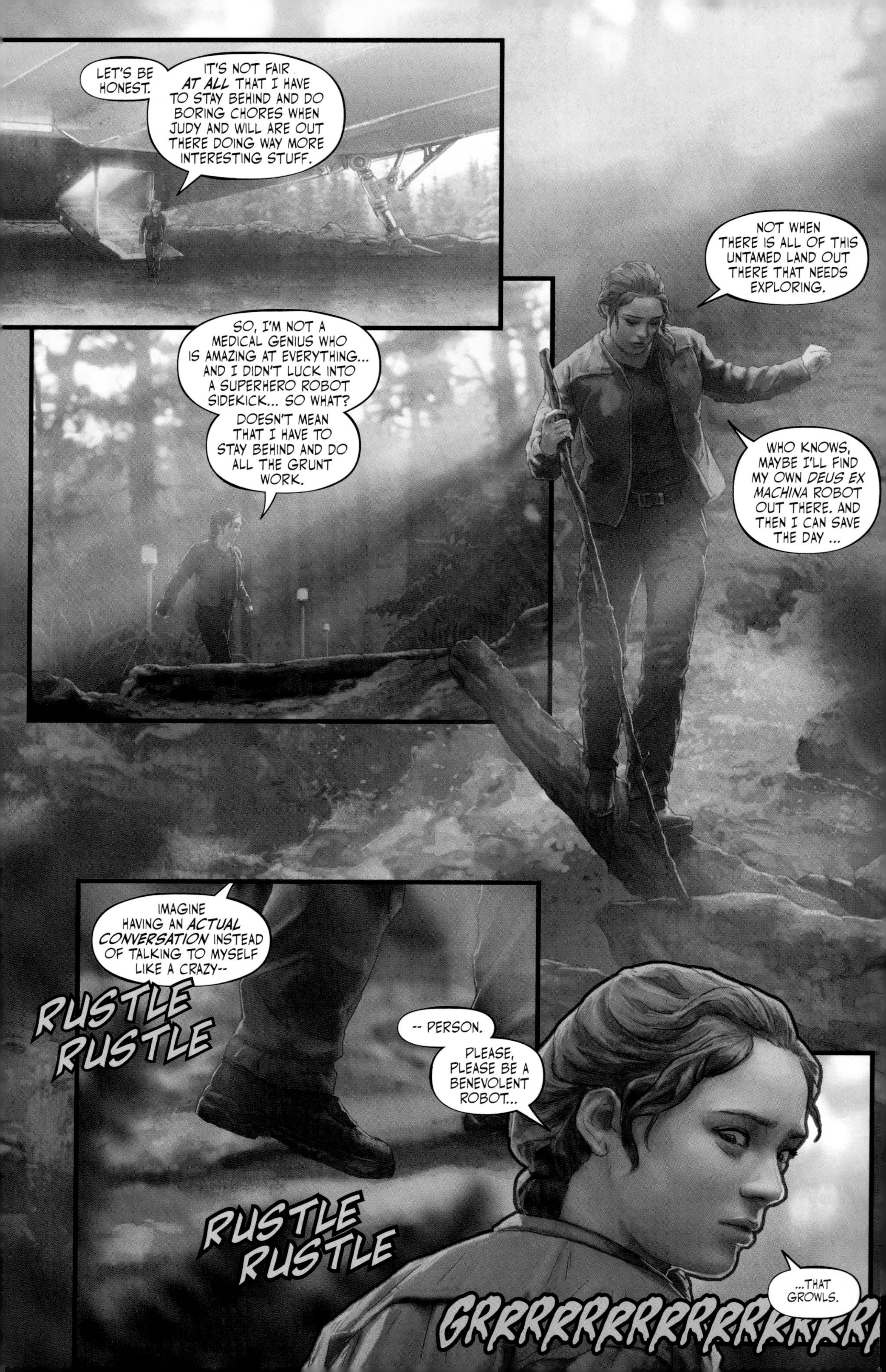
LET'S BE HONEST.
IT'S NOT FAIR *AT ALL* THAT I HAVE TO STAY BEHIND AND DO BORING CHORES WHEN JUDY AND WILL ARE OUT THERE DOING WAY MORE INTERESTING STUFF.
NOT WHEN THERE IS ALL OF THIS UNTAMED LAND OUT THERE THAT NEEDS EXPLORING.
SO, I'M NOT A MEDICAL GENIUS WHO IS AMAZING AT EVERYTHING... AND I DIDN'T LUCK INTO A SUPERHERO ROBOT SIDEKICK... SO WHAT?
DOESN'T MEAN THAT I HAVE TO STAY BEHIND AND DO ALL THE GRUNT WORK.
WHO KNOWS, MAYBE I'LL FIND MY OWN *DEUS EX MACHINA* ROBOT OUT THERE. AND THEN I CAN SAVE THE DAY ...
IMAGINE HAVING AN *ACTUAL CONVERSATION* INSTEAD OF TALKING TO MYSELF LIKE A CRAZY--
RUSTLE RUSTLE
-- PERSON.
PLEASE, PLEASE BE A BENEVOLENT ROBOT...
RUSTLE RUSTLE
...THAT GROWLS.
GRRRRRRRRRRRRRRR

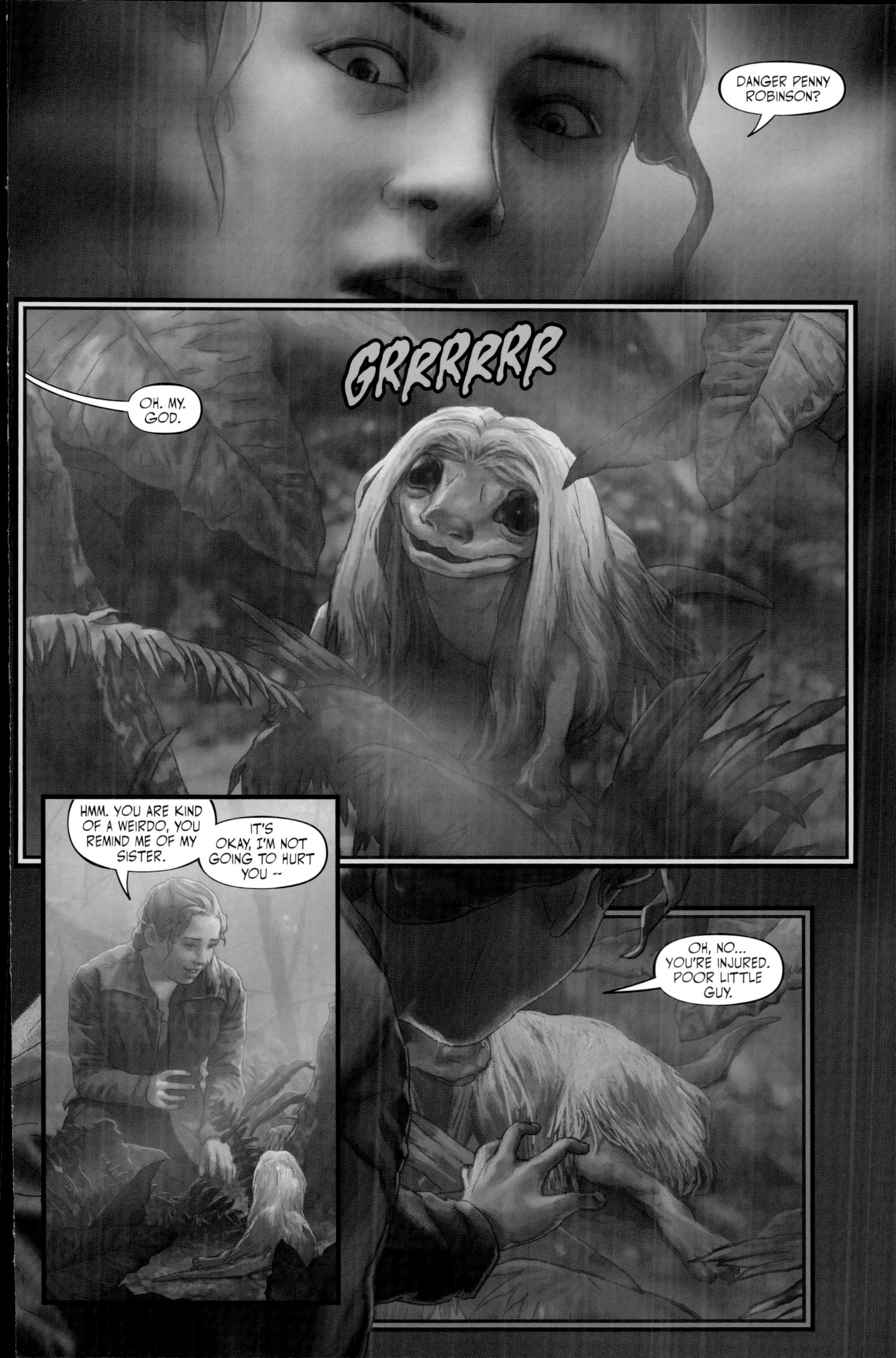
DANGER PENNY ROBINSON?
GRRRRRR
OH. MY. GOD.
HMM. YOU ARE KIND OF A WEIRDO, YOU REMIND ME OF MY SISTER.
IT'S OKAY, I'M NOT GOING TO HURT YOU --
OH, NO... YOU'RE INJURED. POOR LITTLE GUY.

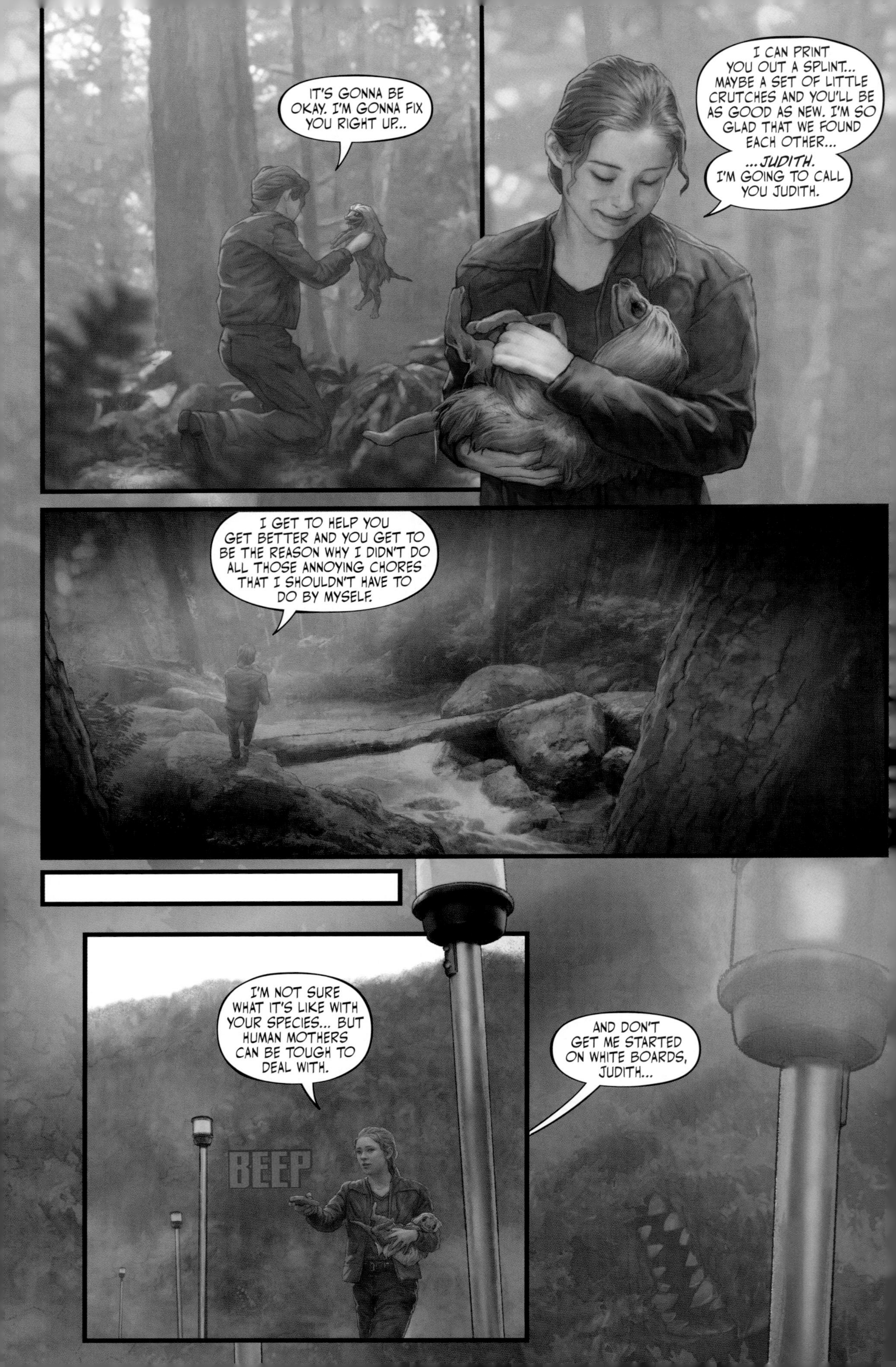
IT'S GONNA BE OKAY. I'M GONNA FIX YOU RIGHT UP...
I CAN PRINT YOU OUT A SPLINT... MAYBE A SET OF LITTLE CRUTCHES AND YOU'LL BE AS GOOD AS NEW. I'M SO GLAD THAT WE FOUND EACH OTHER...
...JUDITH. I'M GOING TO CALL YOU JUDITH.
I GET TO HELP YOU GET BETTER AND YOU GET TO BE THE REASON WHY I DIDN'T DO ALL THOSE ANNOYING CHORES THAT I SHOULDN'T HAVE TO DO BY MYSELF.
I'M NOT SURE WHAT IT'S LIKE WITH YOUR SPECIES... BUT HUMAN MOTHERS CAN BE TOUGH TO DEAL WITH.
BEEP
AND DON'T GET ME STARTED ON WHITE BOARDS, JUDITH...

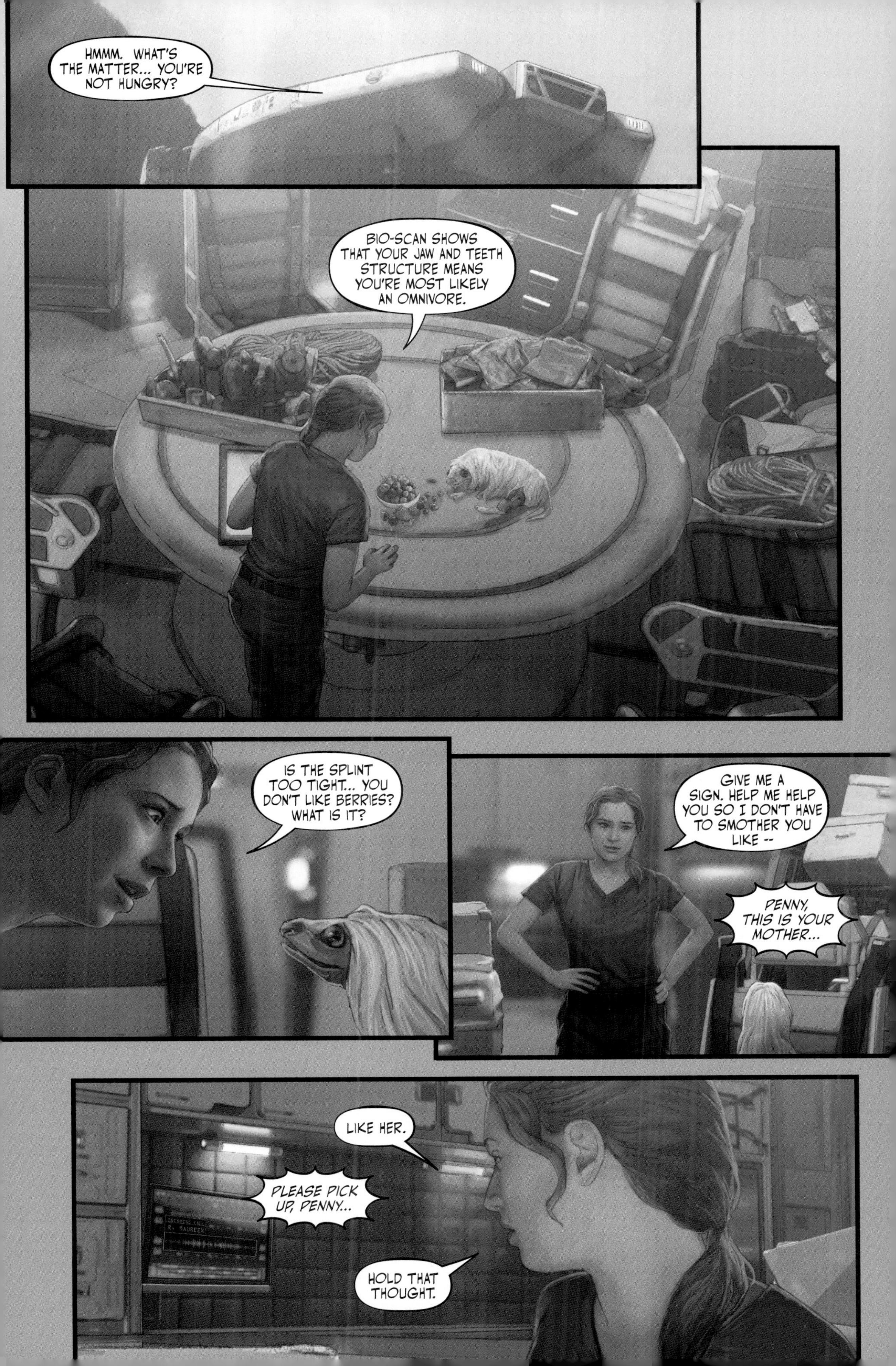
HMMM. WHAT'S THE MATTER... YOU'RE NOT HUNGRY?
BIO-SCAN SHOWS THAT YOUR JAW AND TEETH STRUCTURE MEANS YOU'RE MOST LIKELY AN OMNIVORE.
IS THE SPLINT TOO TIGHT... YOU DON'T LIKE BERRIES? WHAT IS IT?
GIVE ME A SIGN. HELP ME HELP YOU SO I DON'T HAVE TO SMOTHER YOU LIKE --
PENNY, THIS IS YOUR MOTHER...
LIKE HER.
PLEASE PICK UP, PENNY...
HOLD THAT THOUGHT.

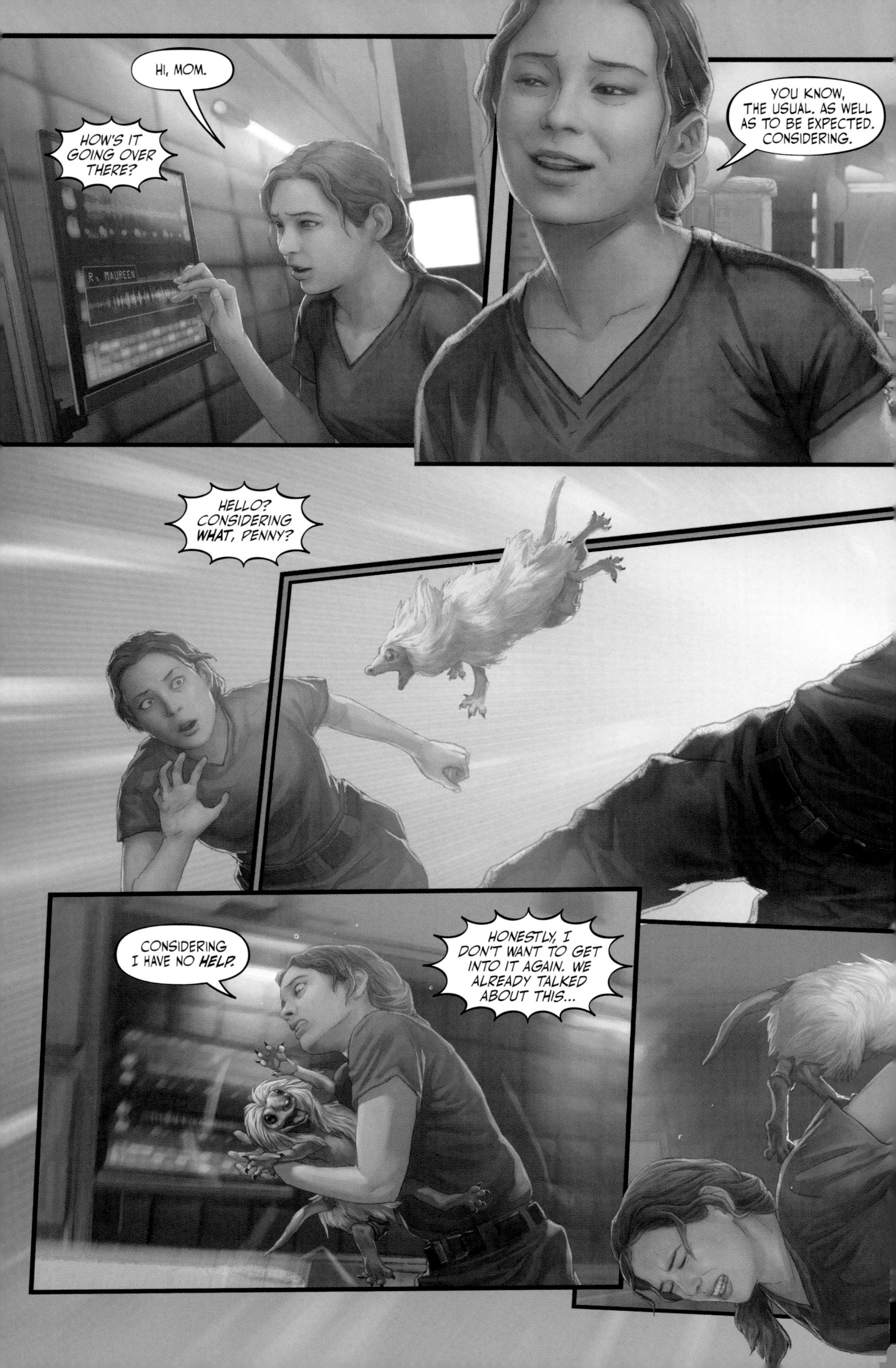
HI, MOM.
HOW'S IT GOING OVER THERE?
R. MAUREEN
YOU KNOW, THE USUAL. AS WELL AS TO BE EXPECTED. CONSIDERING.
HELLO? CONSIDERING *WHAT*, PENNY?
CONSIDERING I HAVE NO *HELP*.
HONESTLY, I DON'T WANT TO GET INTO IT AGAIN. WE ALREADY TALKED ABOUT THIS...

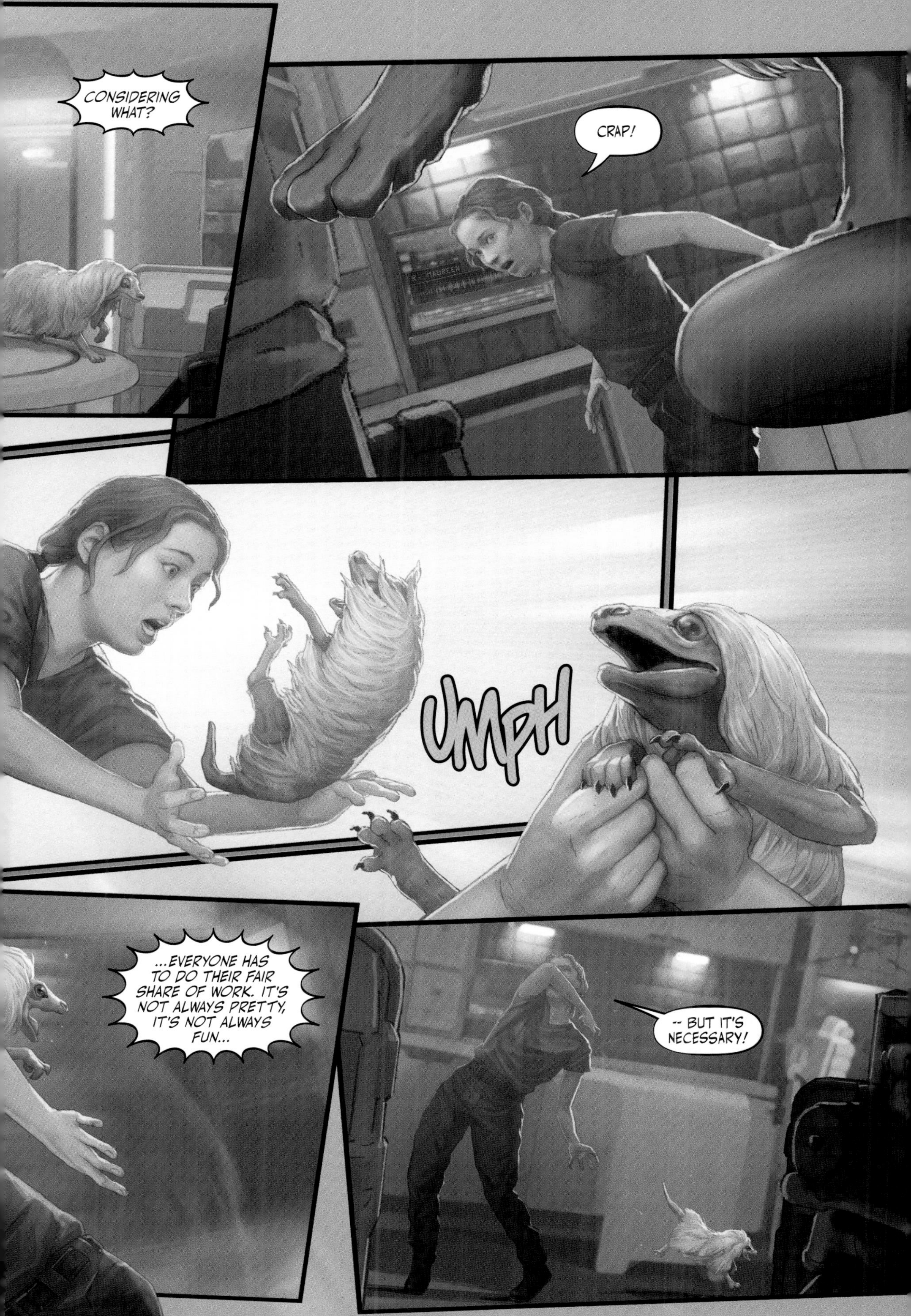
CONSIDERING WHAT?
CRAP!
R - MAUREEN
UMPH
...EVERYONE HAS TO DO THEIR FAIR SHARE OF WORK. IT'S NOT ALWAYS PRETTY, IT'S NOT ALWAYS FUN...
-- BUT IT'S NECESSARY!

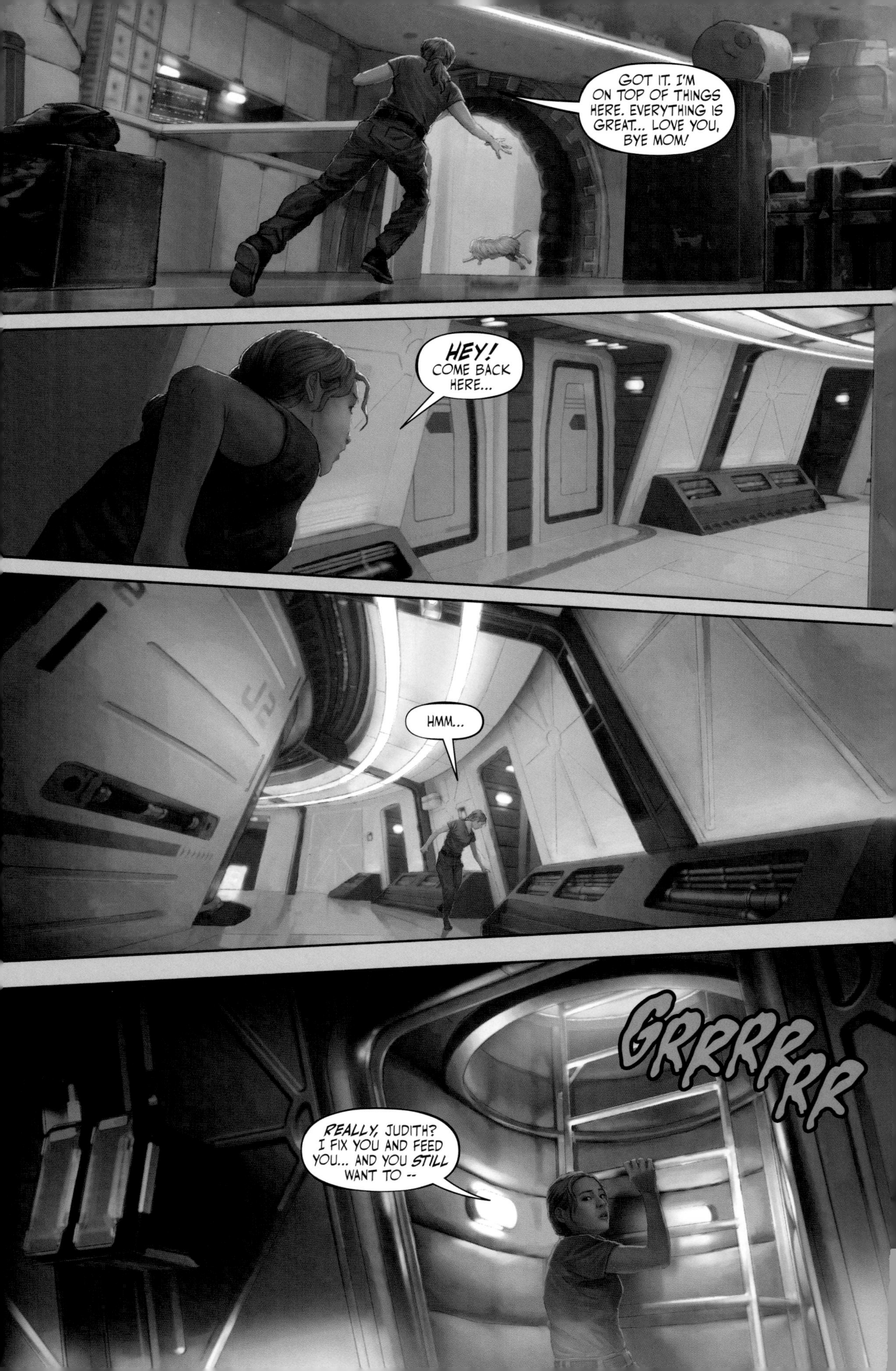
GOT IT. I'M ON TOP OF THINGS HERE. EVERYTHING IS GREAT... LOVE YOU, BYE MOM!
HEY! COME BACK HERE...
HMM...
GRRRRRR
REALLY, JUDITH? I FIX YOU AND FEED YOU... AND YOU STILL WANT TO --

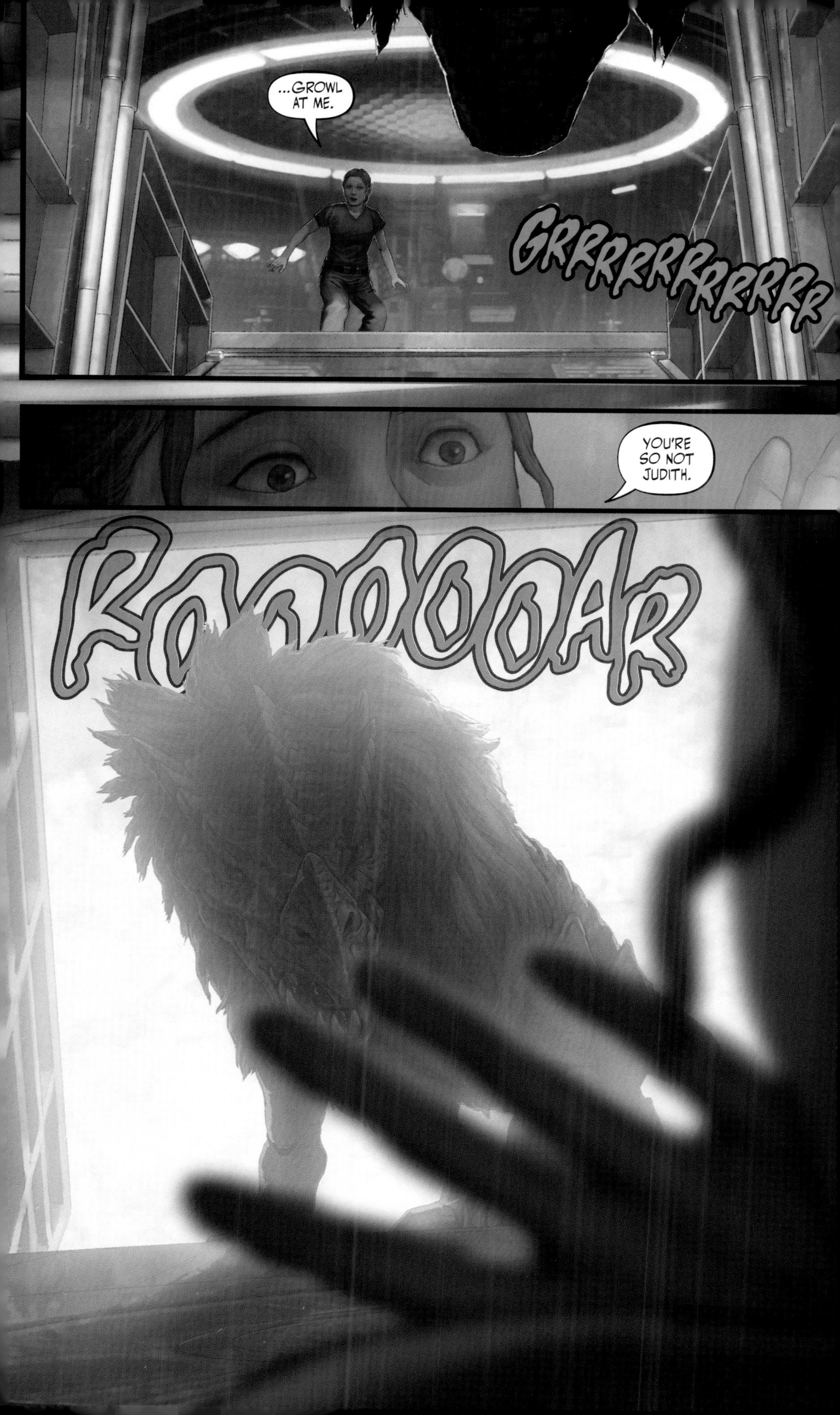
...GROWL AT ME.
GRRRRRRRRRRRR
YOU'RE SO NOT JUDITH.
ROOOOOAR

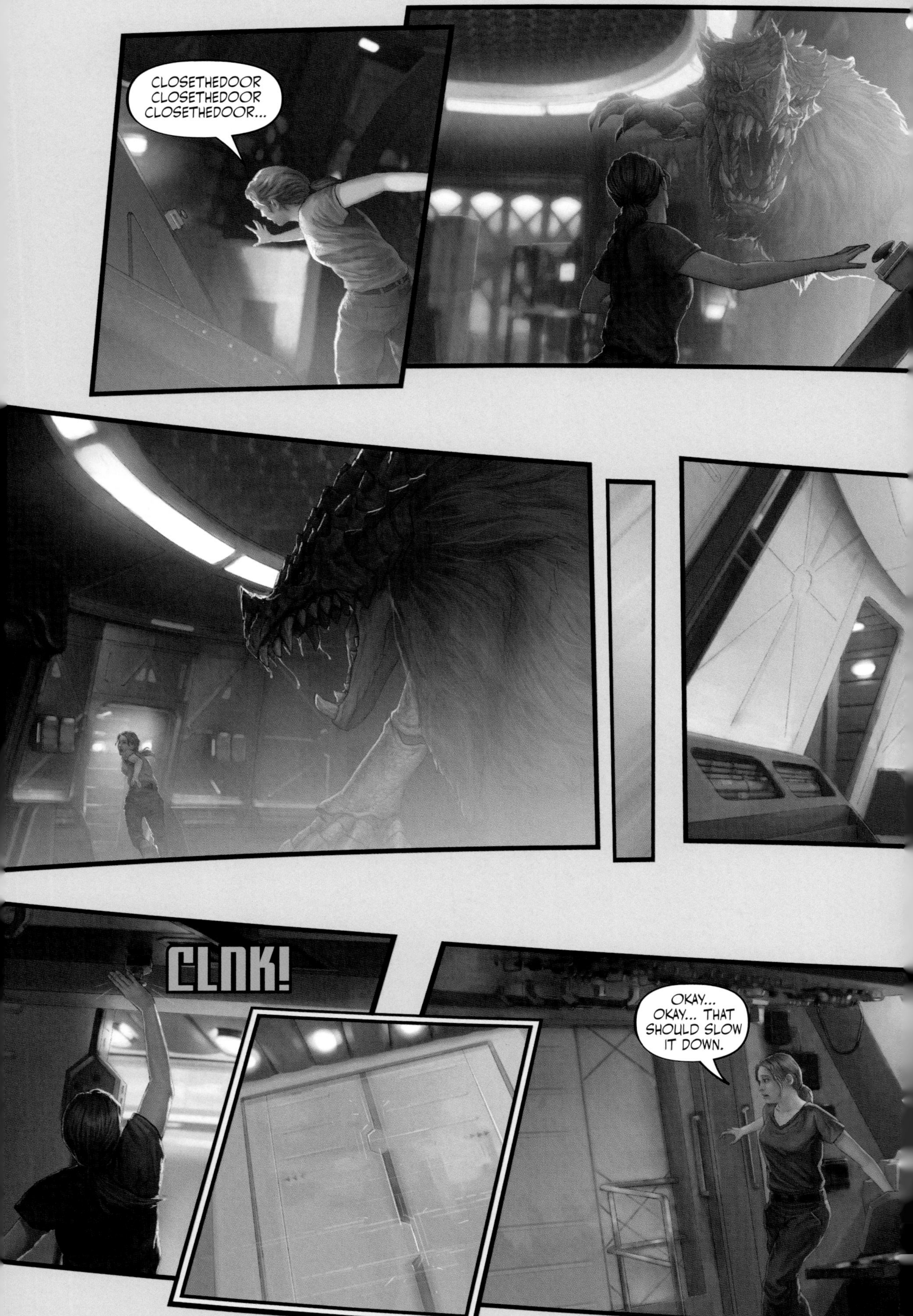
CLOSETHEDOOR
CLOSETHEDOOR
CLOSETHEDOOR...
CLNK!
OKAY... OKAY... THAT SHOULD SLOW IT DOWN.

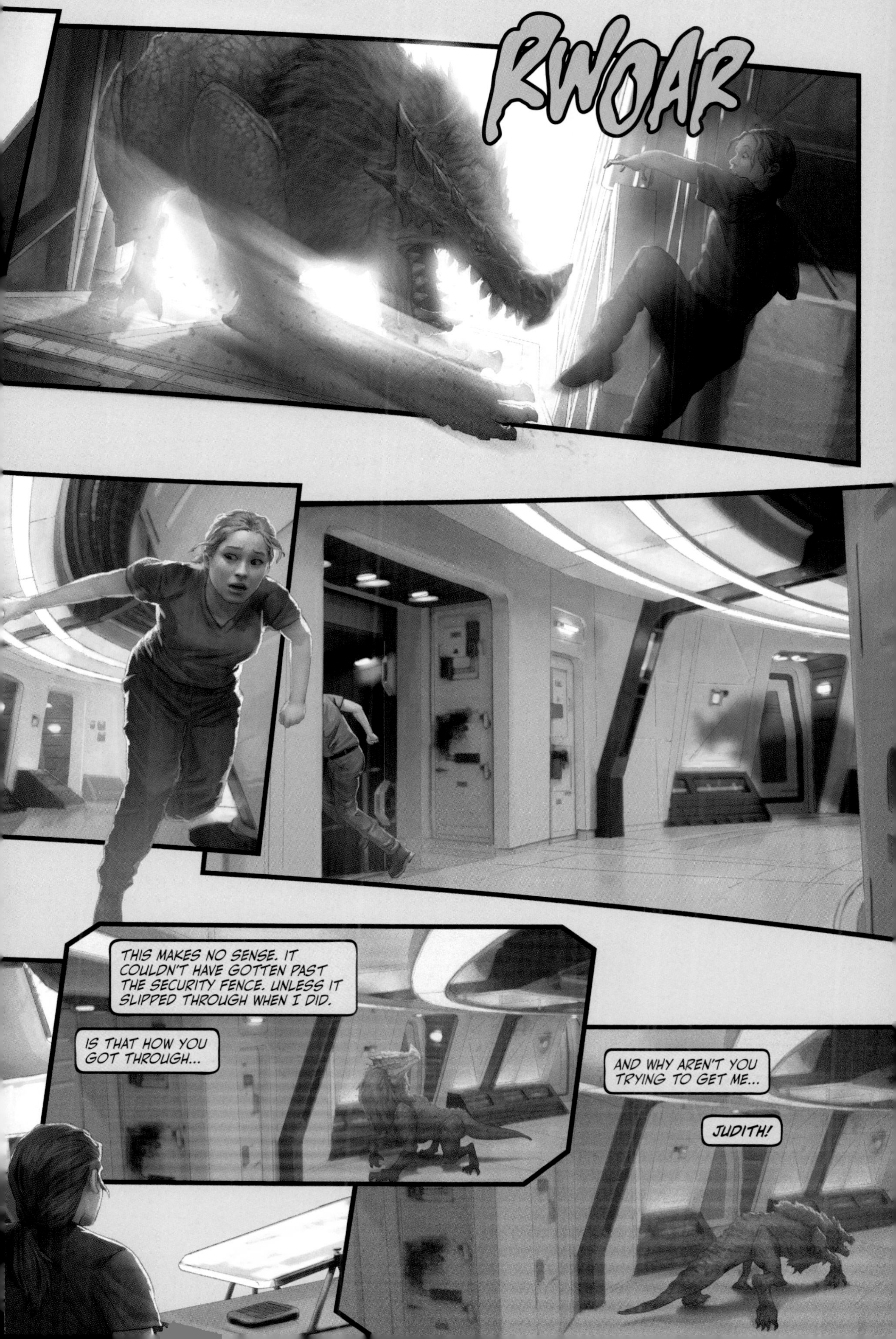
RWOAR
THIS MAKES NO SENSE. IT COULDN'T HAVE GOTTEN PAST THE SECURITY FENCE. UNLESS IT SLIPPED THROUGH WHEN I DID.
IS THAT HOW YOU GOT THROUGH...
AND WHY AREN'T YOU TRYING TO GET ME...
JUDITH!

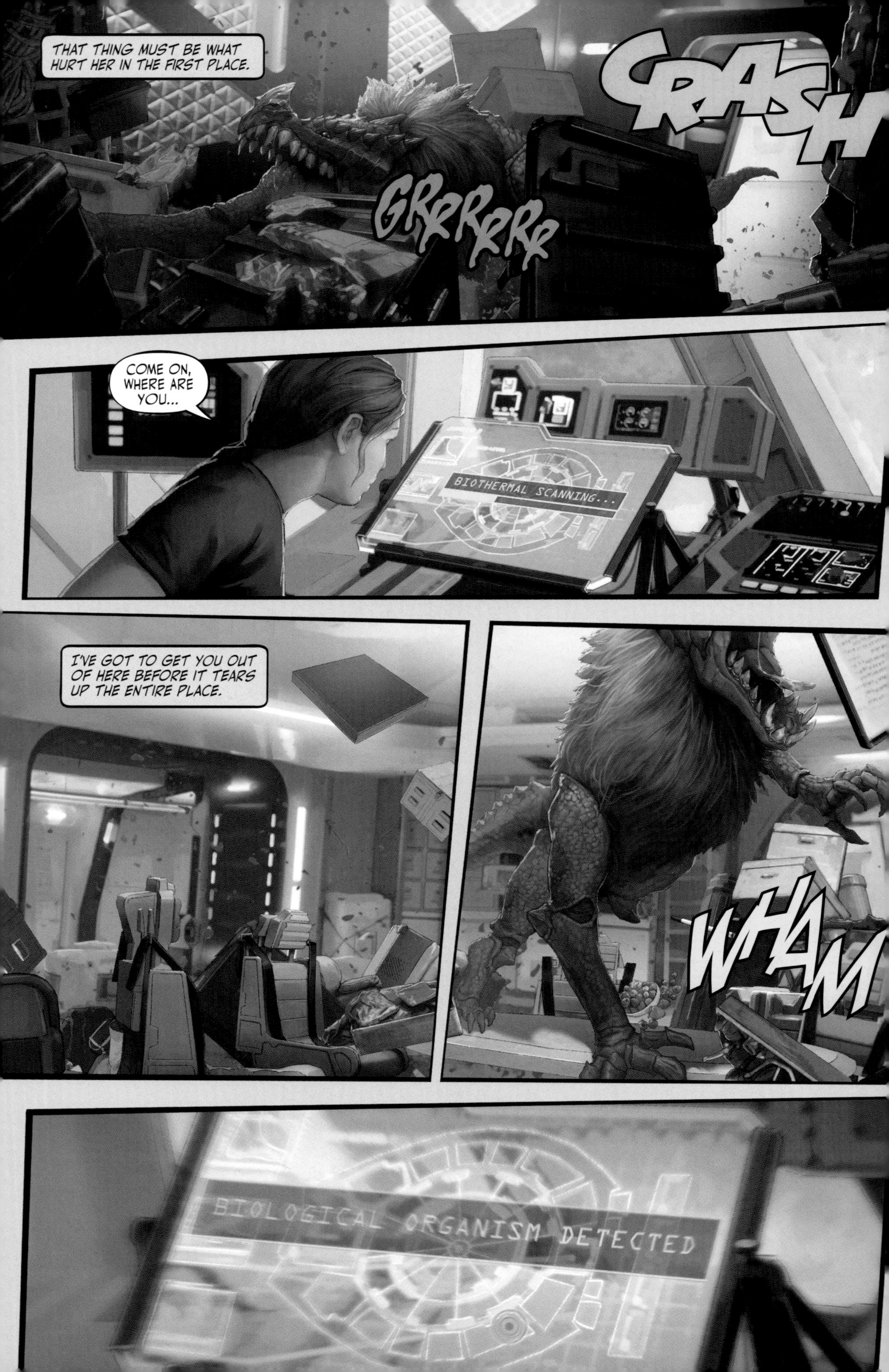
THAT THING MUST BE WHAT HURT HER IN THE FIRST PLACE.
CRASH
GRRRRRR
COME ON, WHERE ARE YOU...
BIOTHERMAL SCANNING...
I'VE GOT TO GET YOU OUT OF HERE BEFORE IT TEARS UP THE ENTIRE PLACE.
WHAM
BIOLOGICAL ORGANISM DETECTED

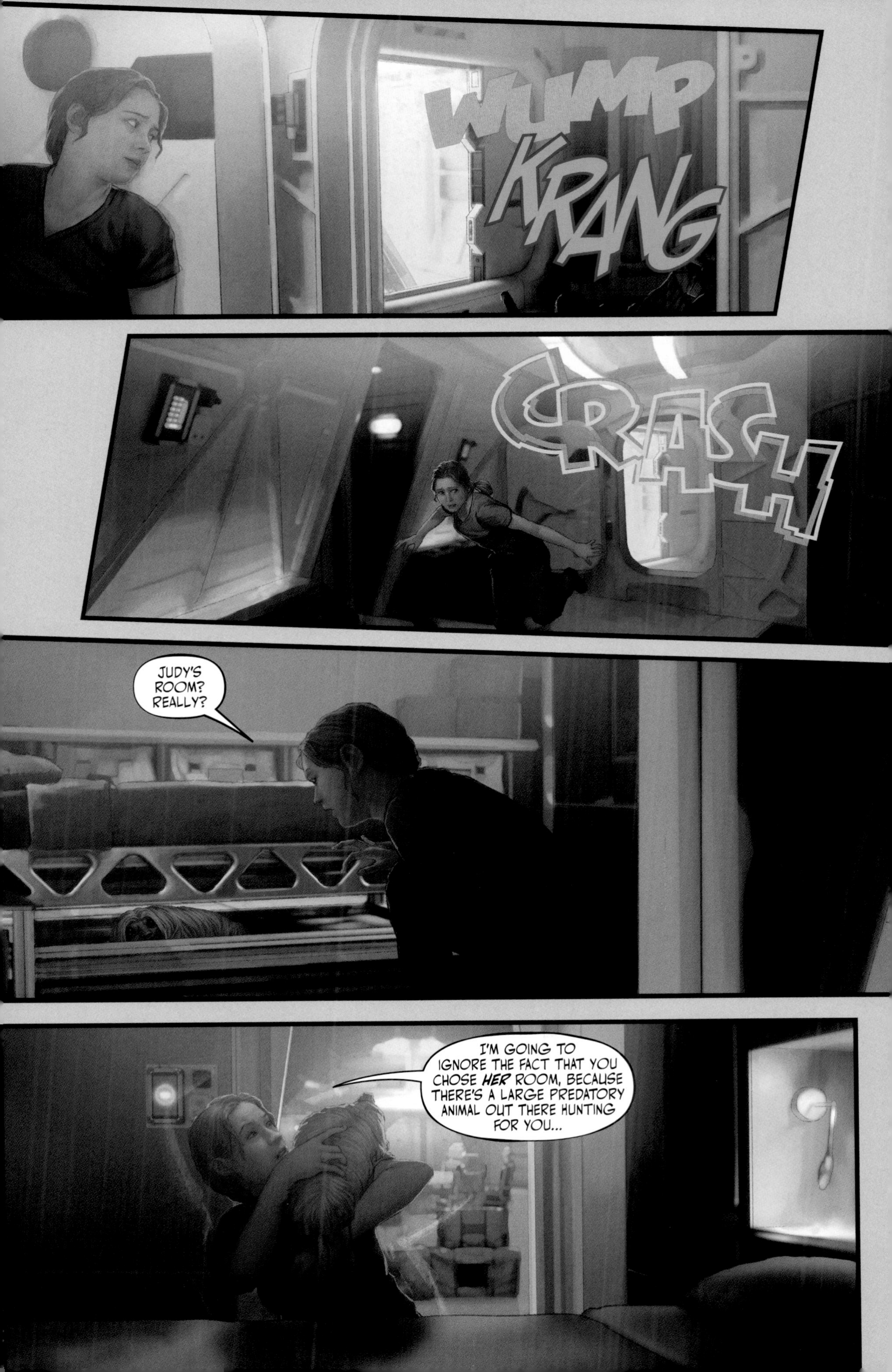
WUMP
KRANG
CRASH
JUDY'S ROOM? REALLY?
I'M GOING TO IGNORE THE FACT THAT YOU CHOSE *HER* ROOM, BECAUSE THERE'S A LARGE PREDATORY ANIMAL OUT THERE HUNTING FOR YOU...

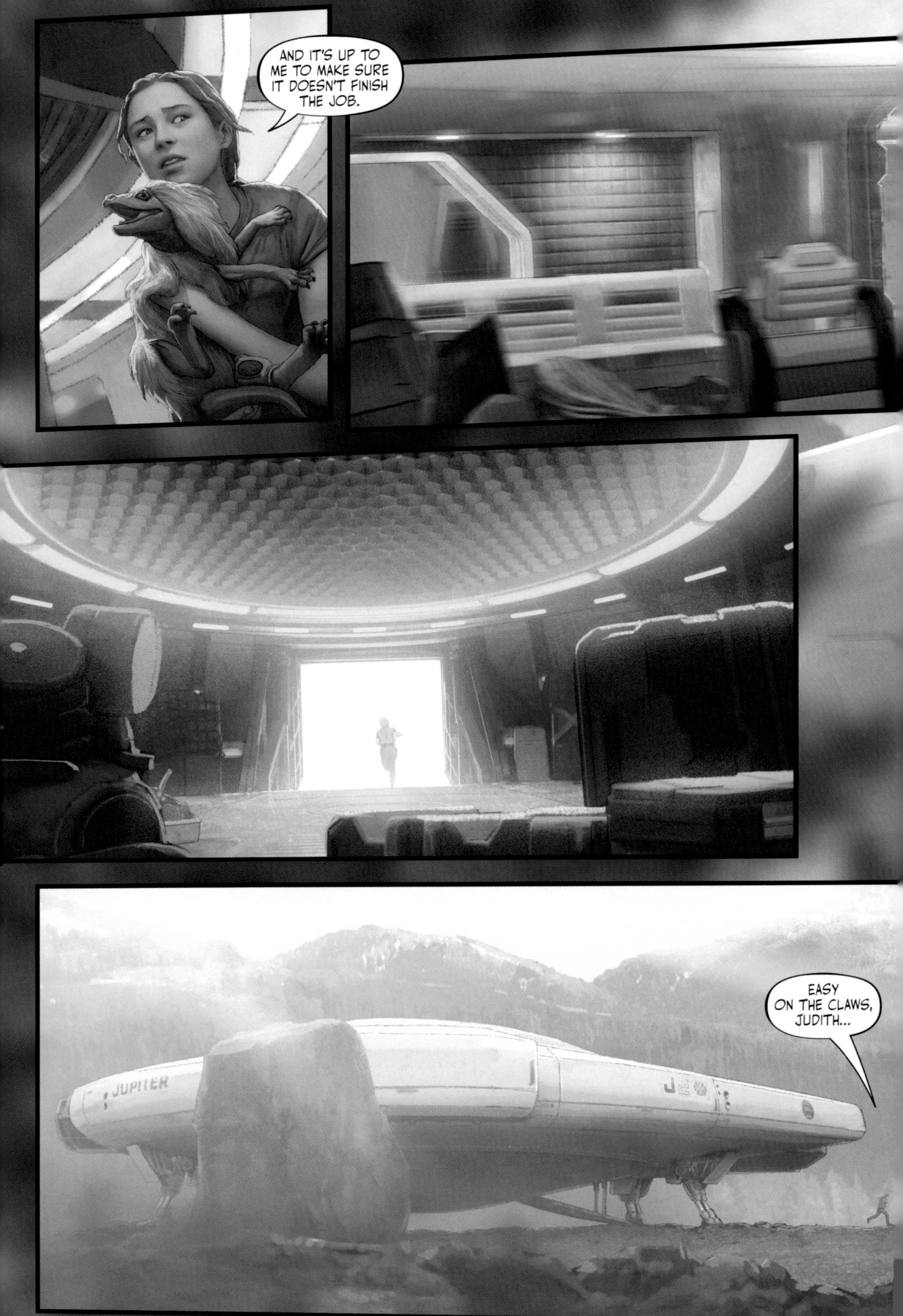
AND IT'S UP TO ME TO MAKE SURE IT DOESN'T FINISH THE JOB.
JUPITER
EASY ON THE CLAWS, JUDITH...

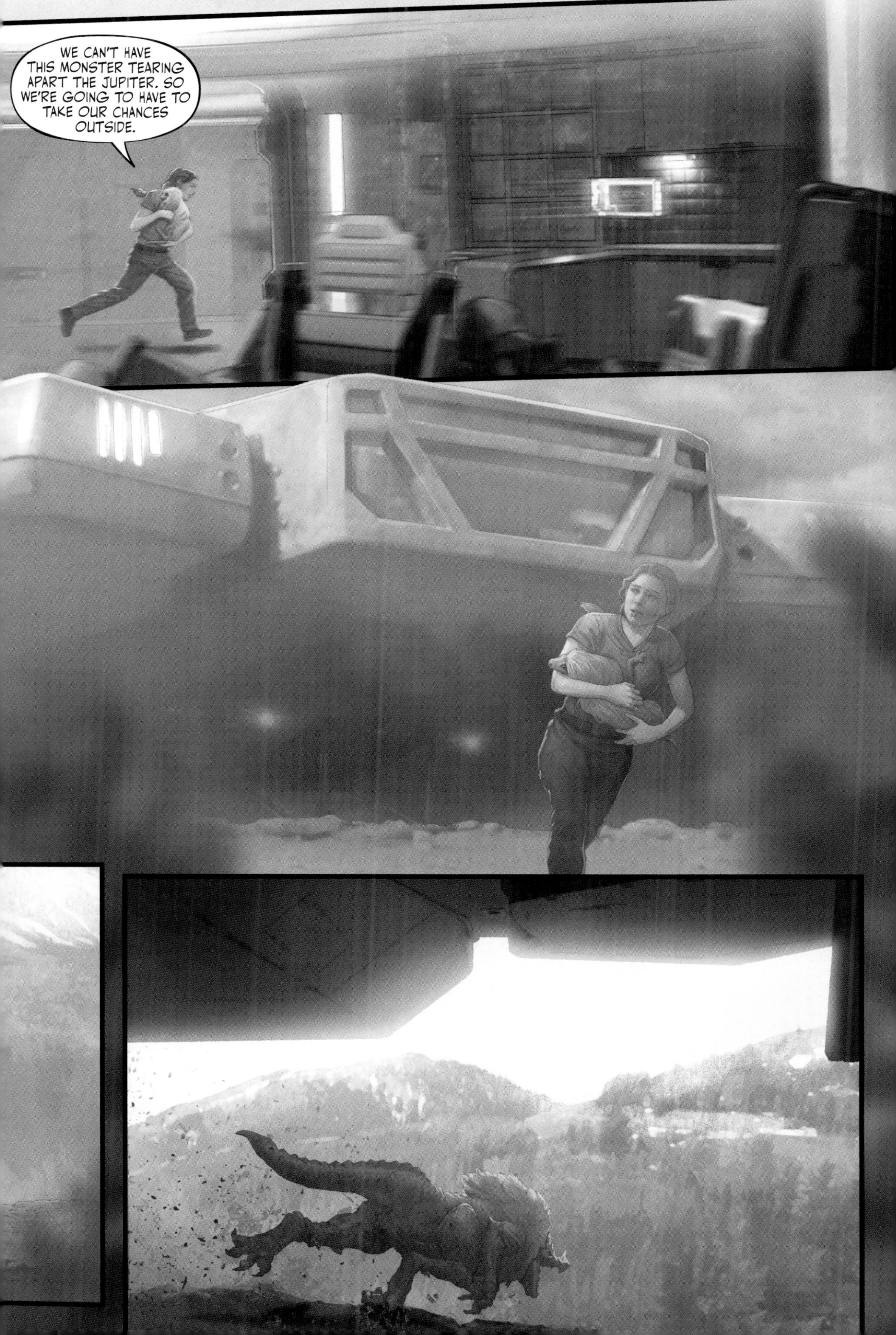
WE CAN'T HAVE THIS MONSTER TEARING APART THE JUPITER. SO WE'RE GOING TO HAVE TO TAKE OUR CHANCES OUTSIDE.

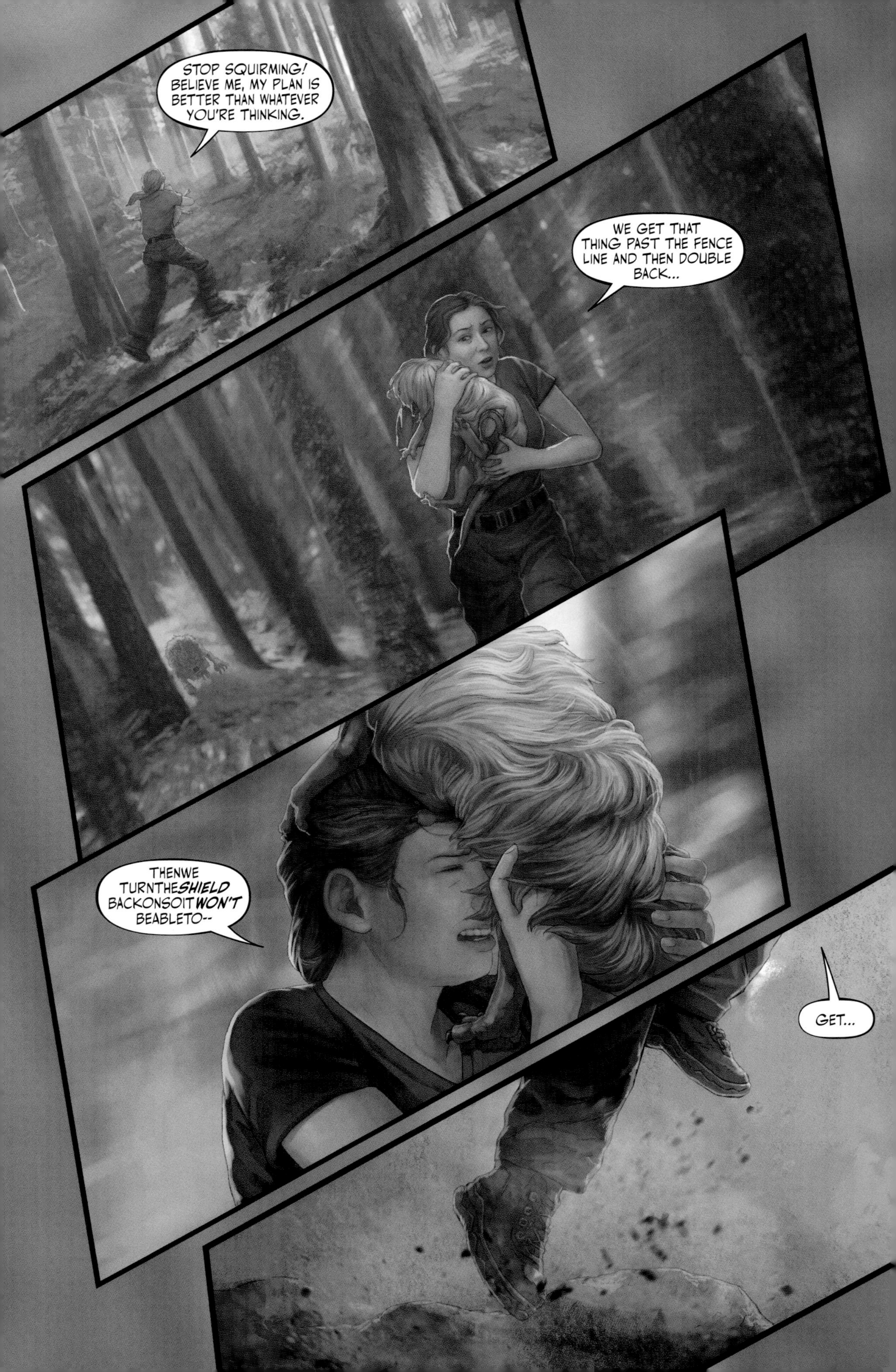
STOP SQUIRMING! BELIEVE ME, MY PLAN IS BETTER THAN WHATEVER YOU'RE THINKING.
WE GET THAT THING PAST THE FENCE LINE AND THEN DOUBLE BACK...
THENWE TURNTHESHIELD BACKONSOIT WON'T BEABLETO--
GET...

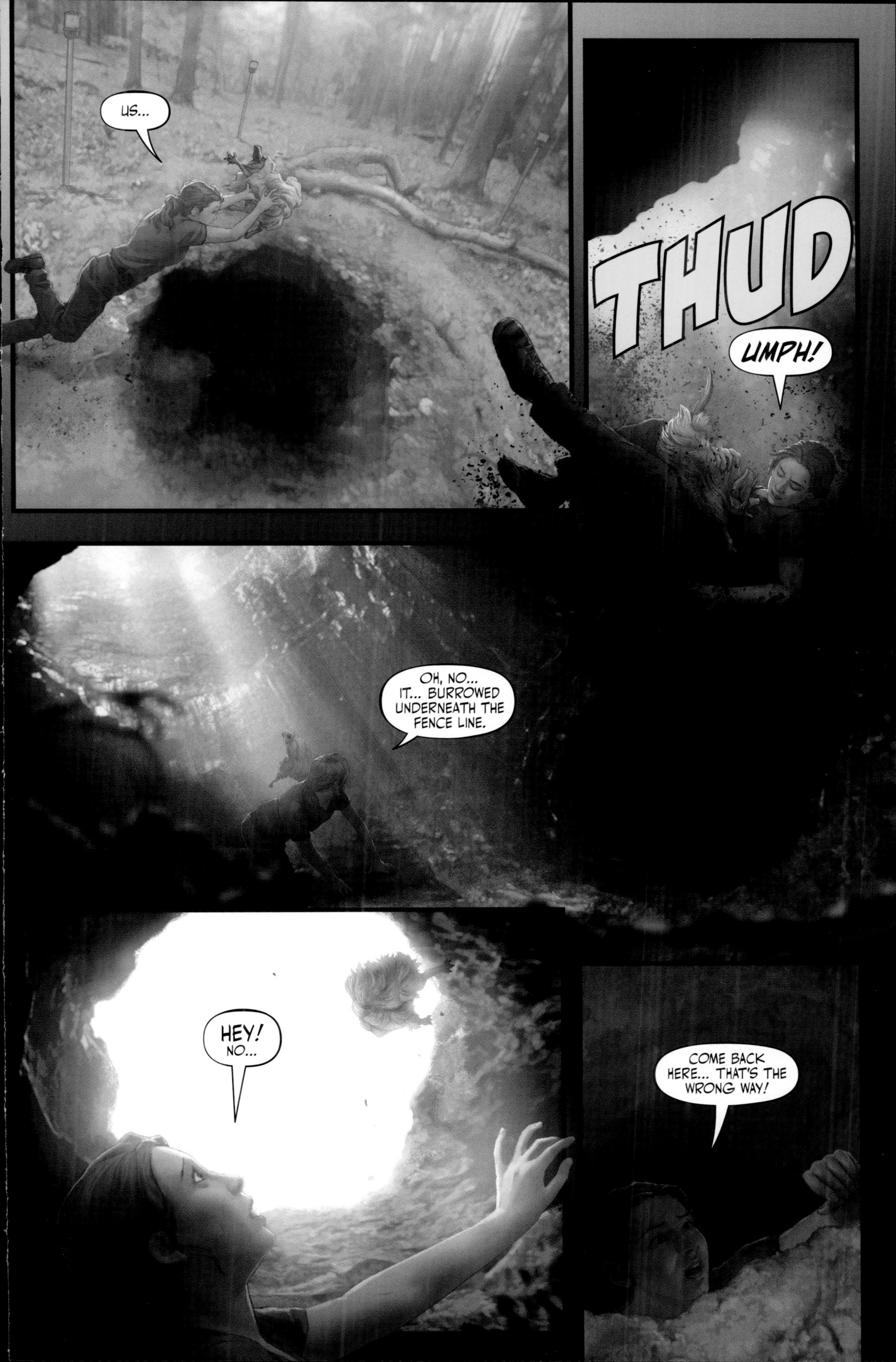
US...
THUD
UMPH!
OH, NO... IT... BURROWED UNDERNEATH THE FENCE LINE.
HEY! NO...
COME BACK HERE... THAT'S THE WRONG WAY!

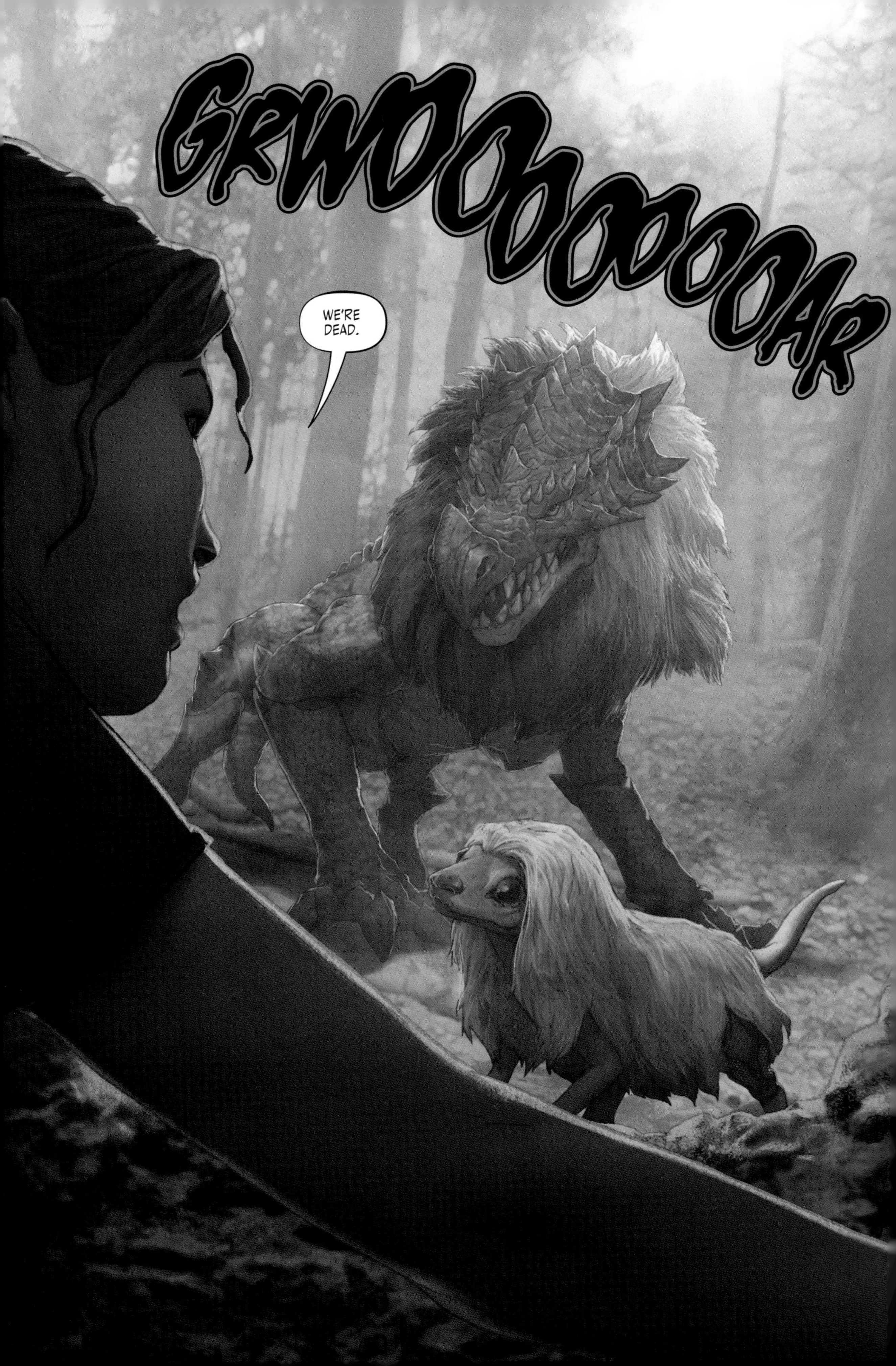
GRWOOOOOOOAR
WE'RE DEAD.

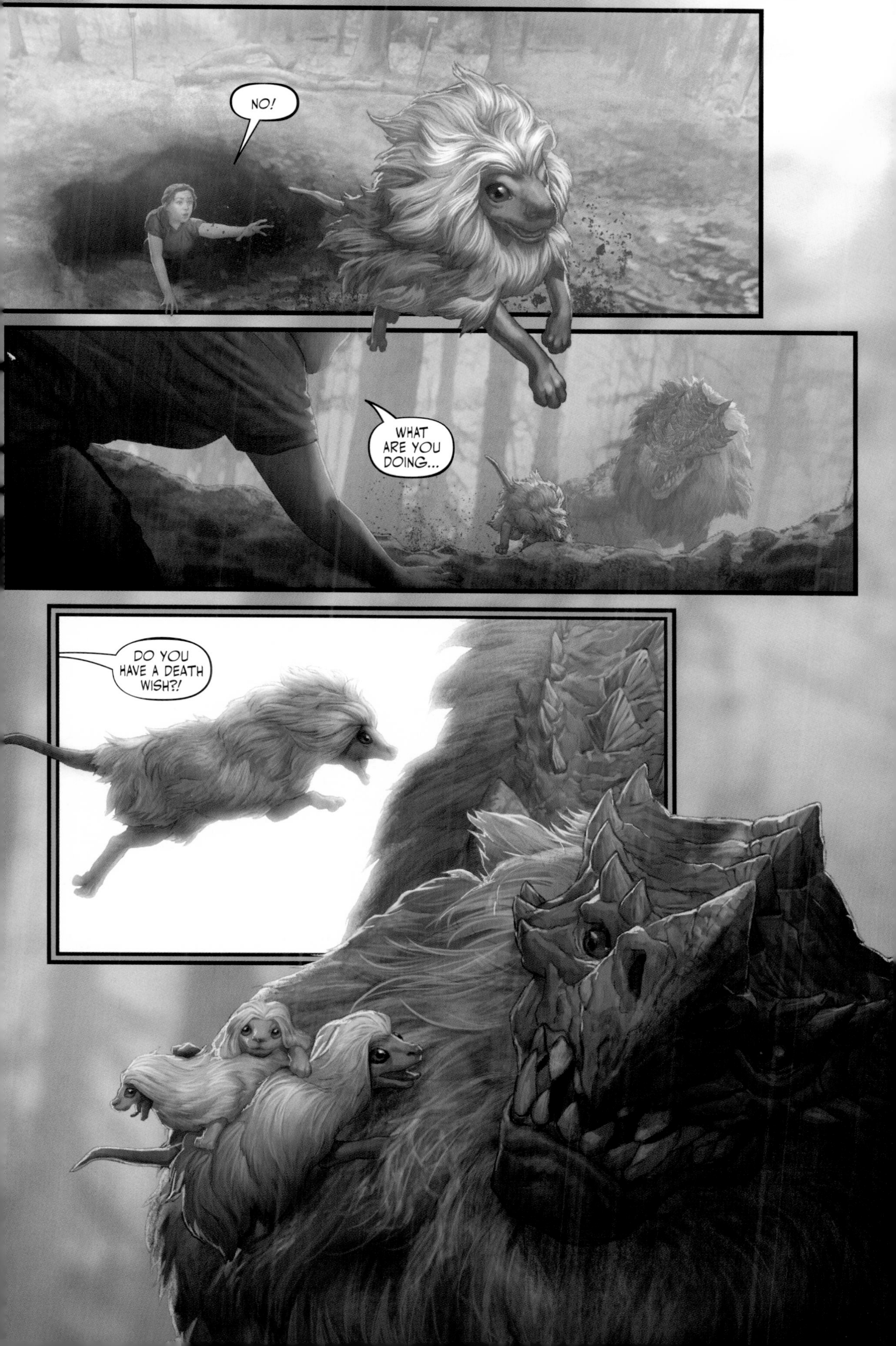
NO!
WHAT ARE YOU DOING...
DO YOU HAVE A DEATH WISH?!

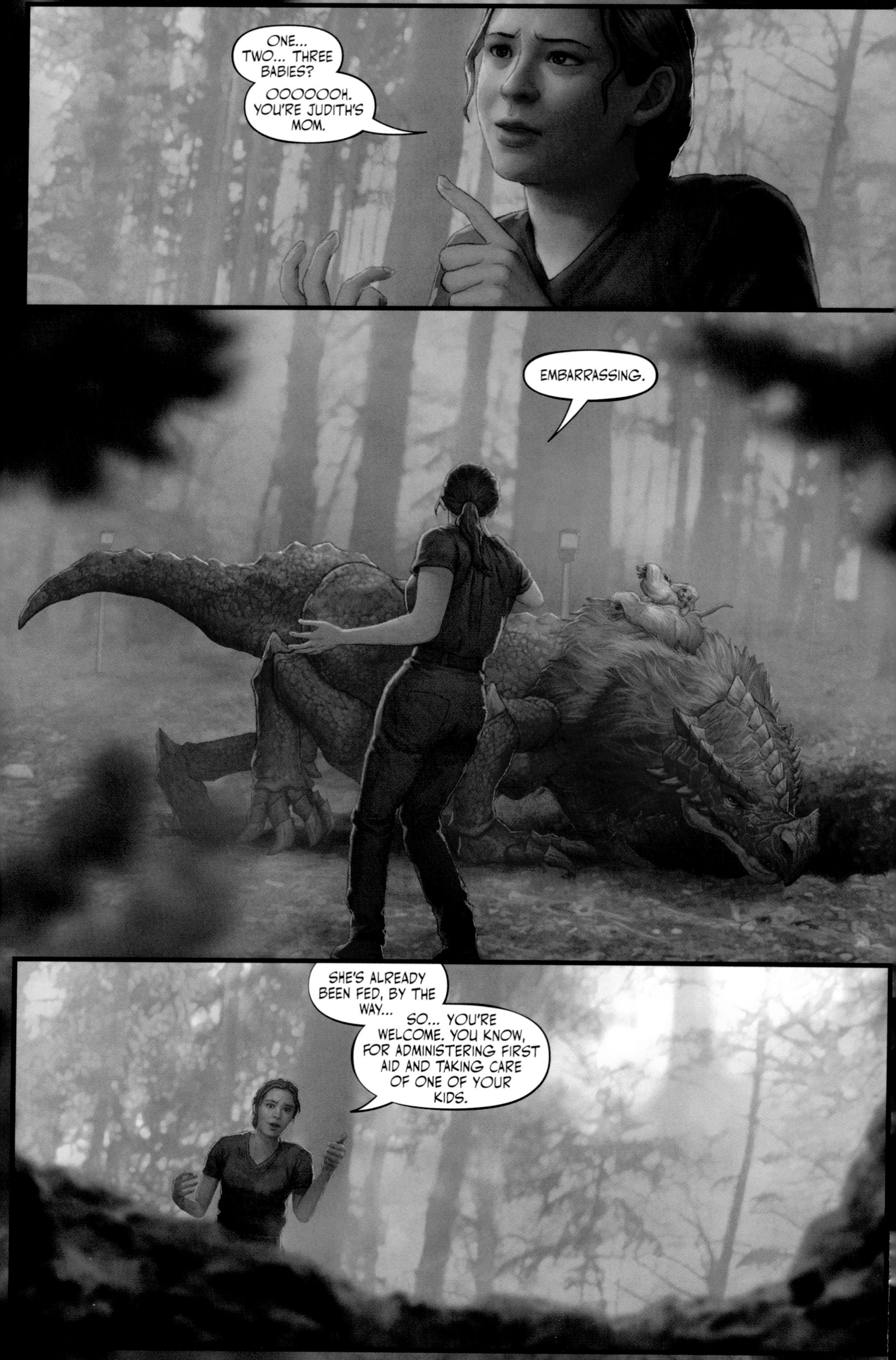
ONE... TWO... THREE BABIES?
OOOOOOH. YOU'RE JUDITH'S MOM.
EMBARRASSING.
SHE'S ALREADY BEEN FED, BY THE WAY...
SO... YOU'RE WELCOME. YOU KNOW, FOR ADMINISTERING FIRST AID AND TAKING CARE OF ONE OF YOUR KIDS.

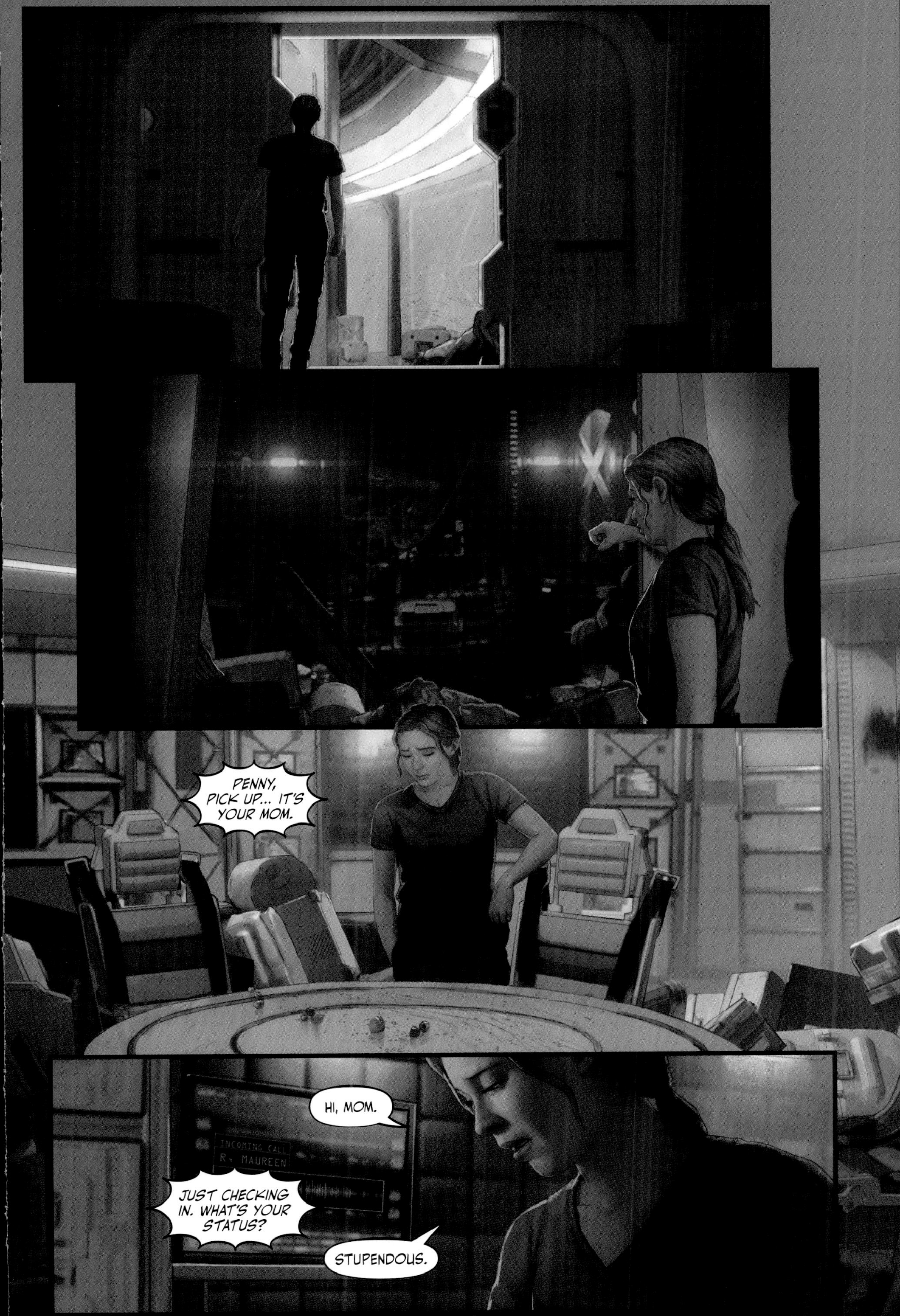
PENNY, PICK UP... IT'S YOUR MOM.
INCOMING CALL
R. MAUREEN
HI, MOM.
JUST CHECKING IN. WHAT'S YOUR STATUS?
STUPENDOUS.

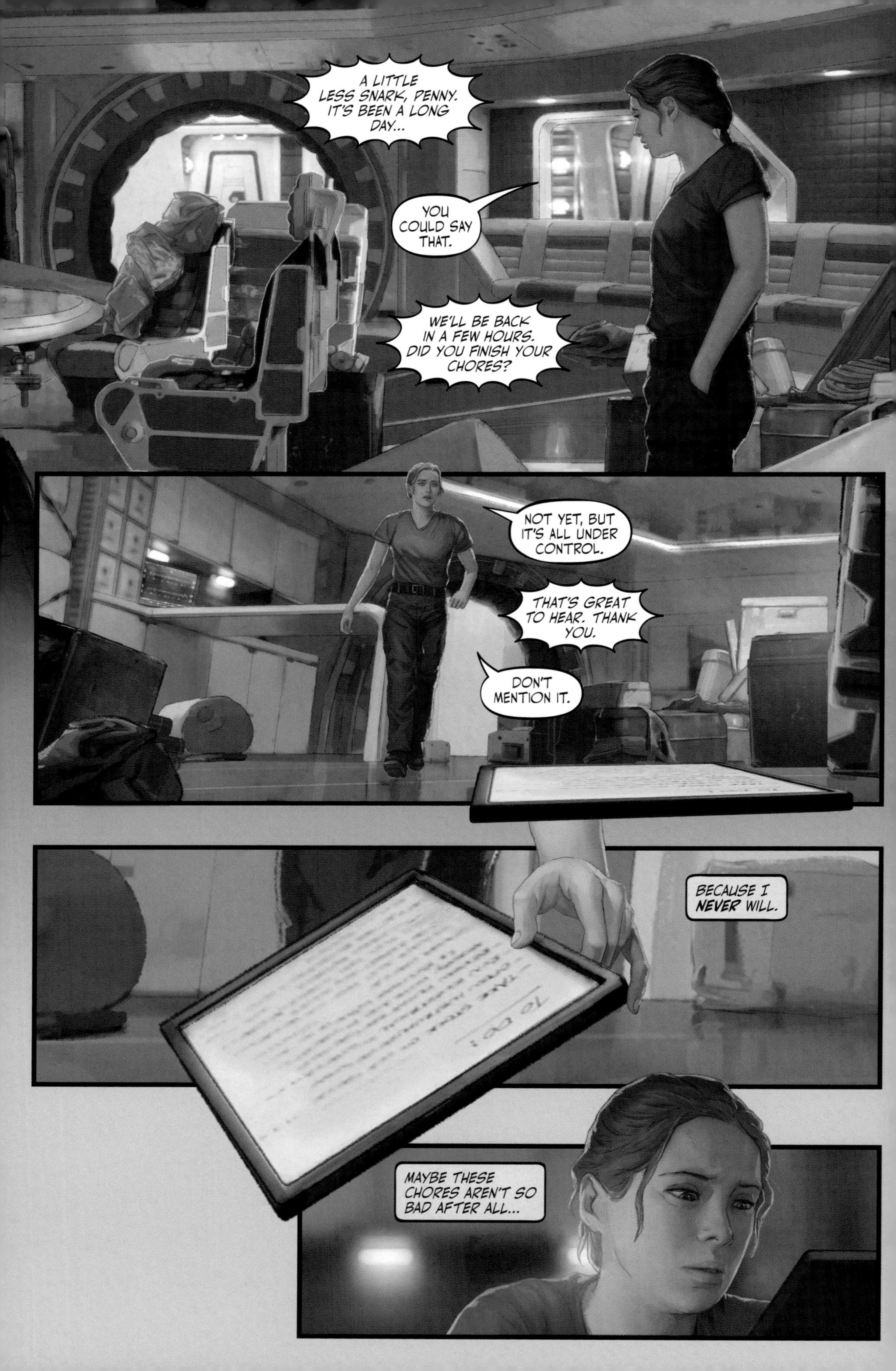
A LITTLE LESS SNARK, PENNY. IT'S BEEN A LONG DAY...
YOU COULD SAY THAT.
WE'LL BE BACK IN A FEW HOURS. DID YOU FINISH YOUR CHORES?
NOT YET, BUT IT'S ALL UNDER CONTROL.
THAT'S GREAT TO HEAR. THANK YOU.
DON'T MENTION IT.
BECAUSE I NEVER WILL.
TO DO:
MAYBE THESE CHORES AREN'T SO BAD AFTER ALL...

BONUS MATERIALS

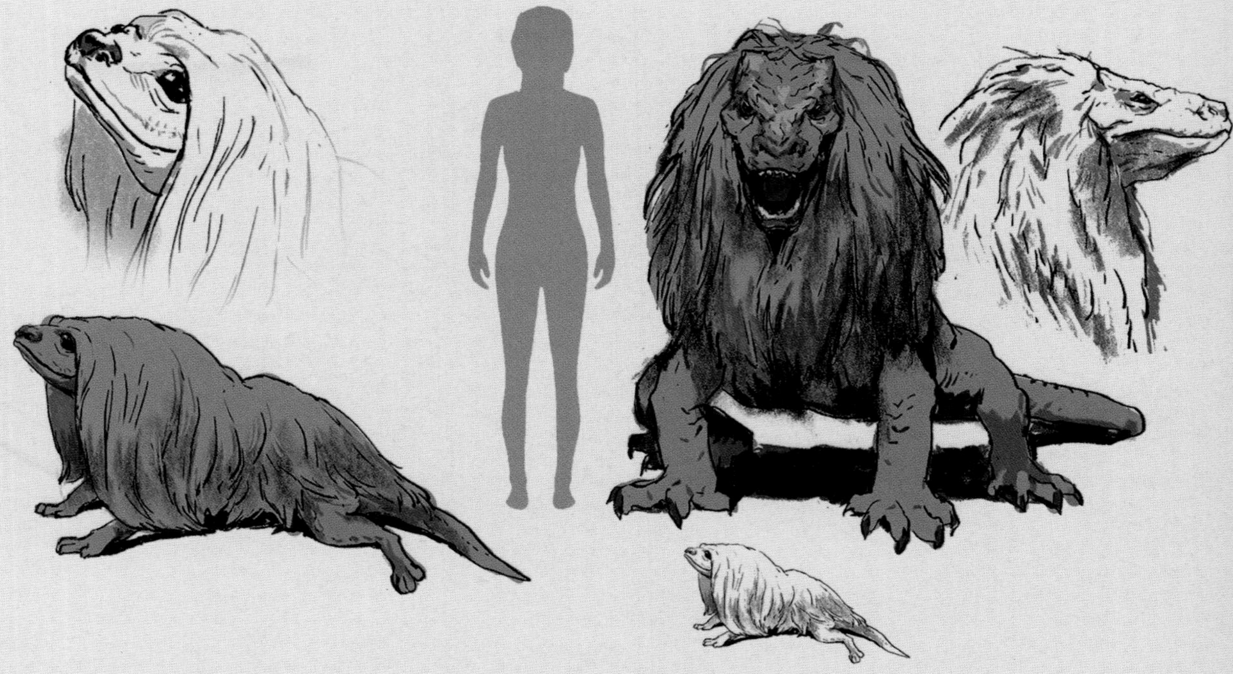

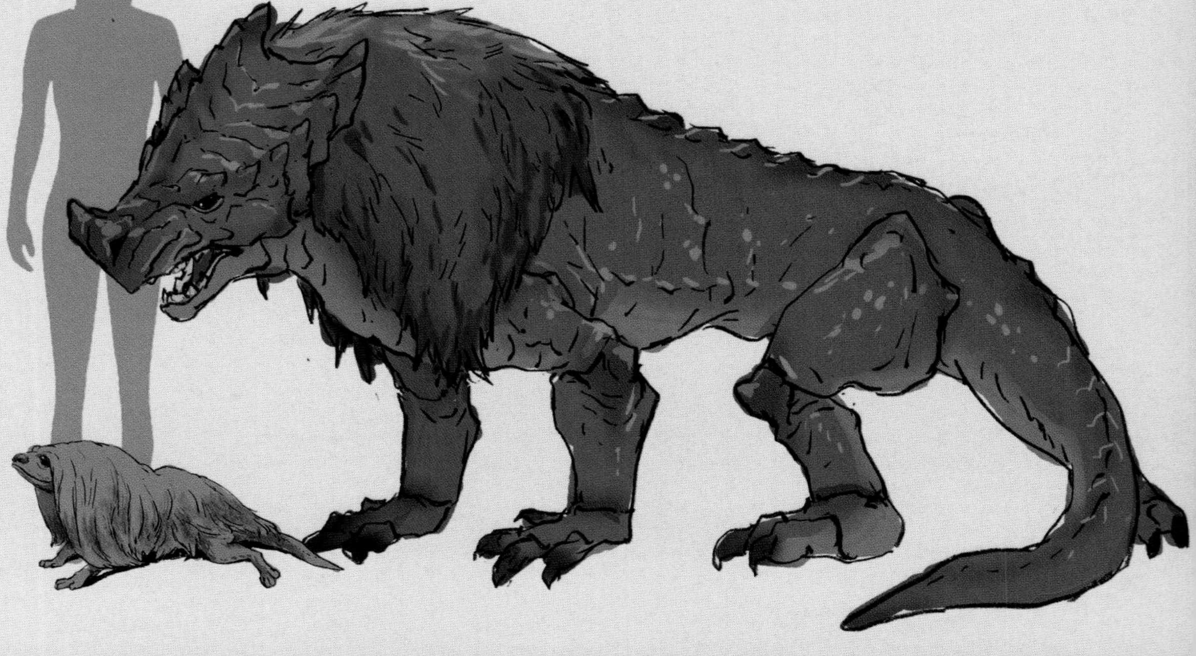

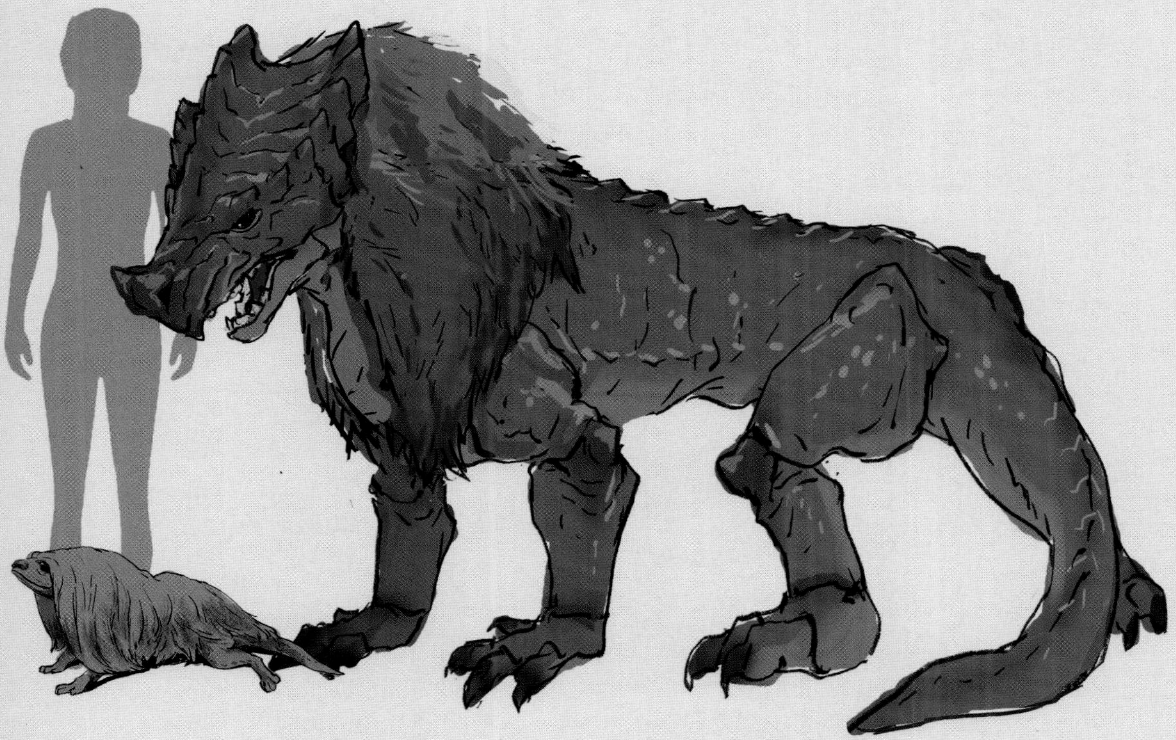

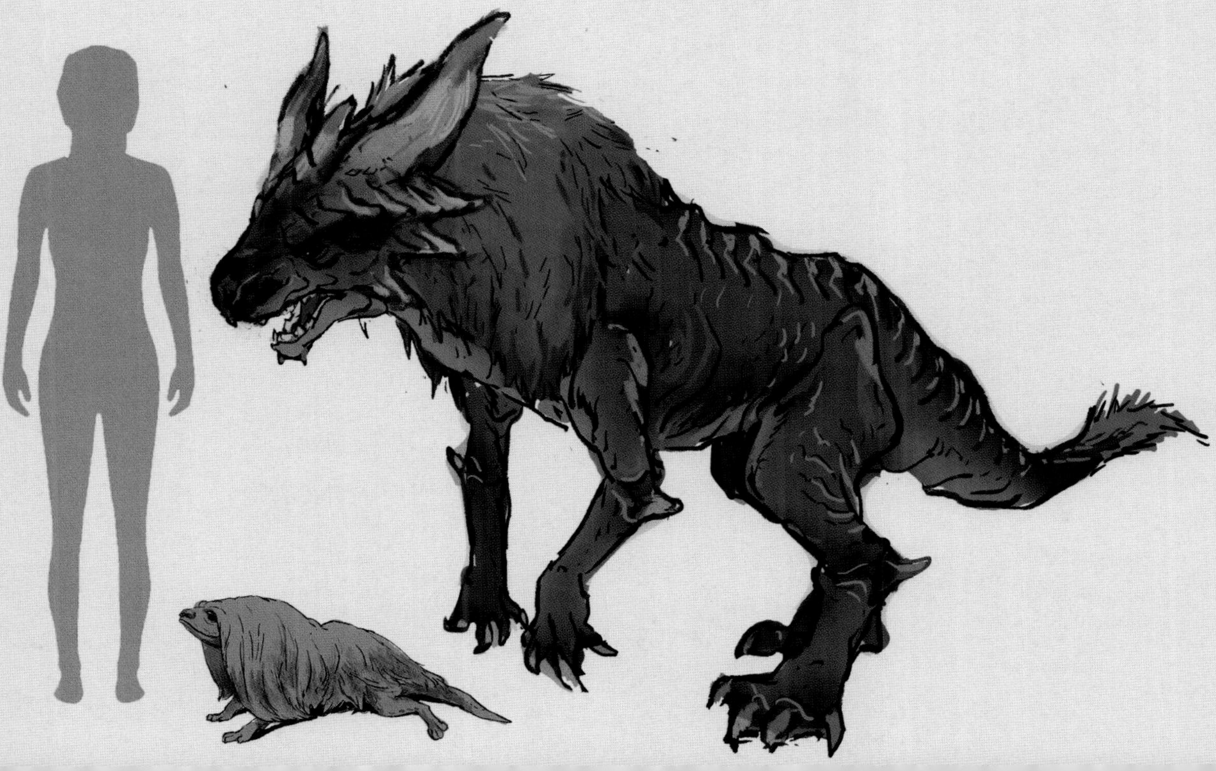

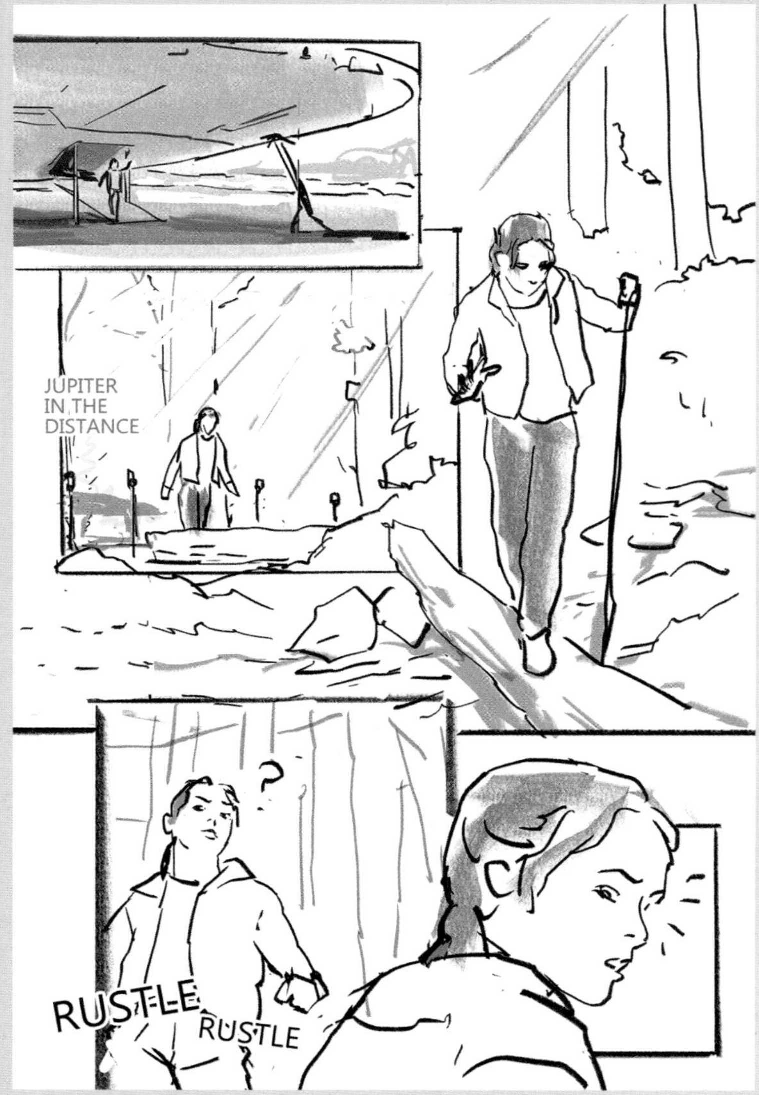
JUPITER
IN THE
DISTANCE
RUSTLE
RUSTLE
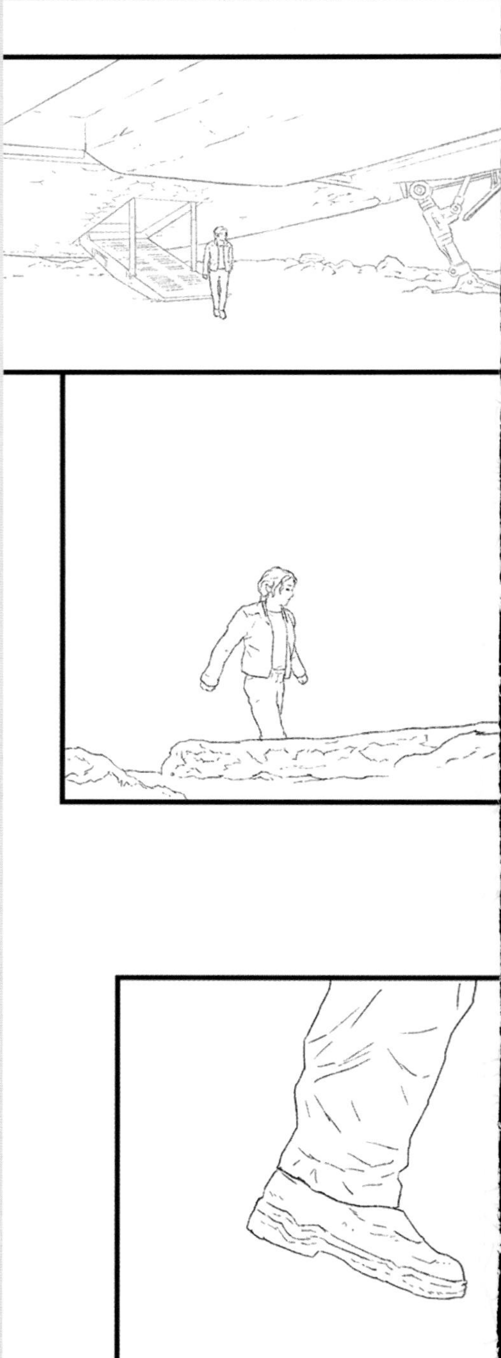

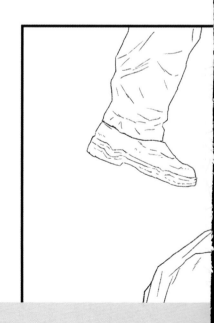

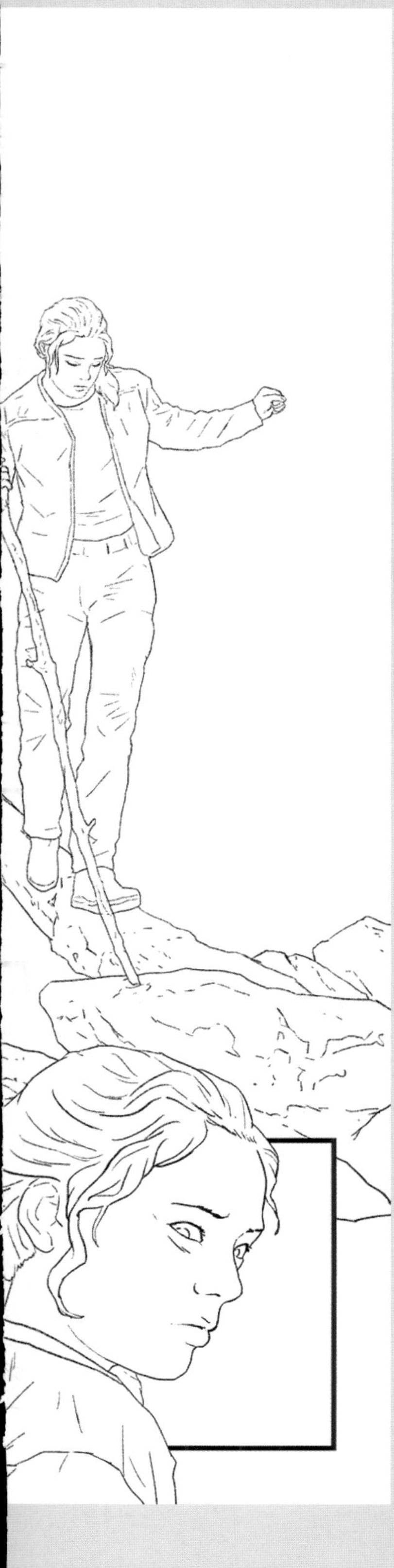

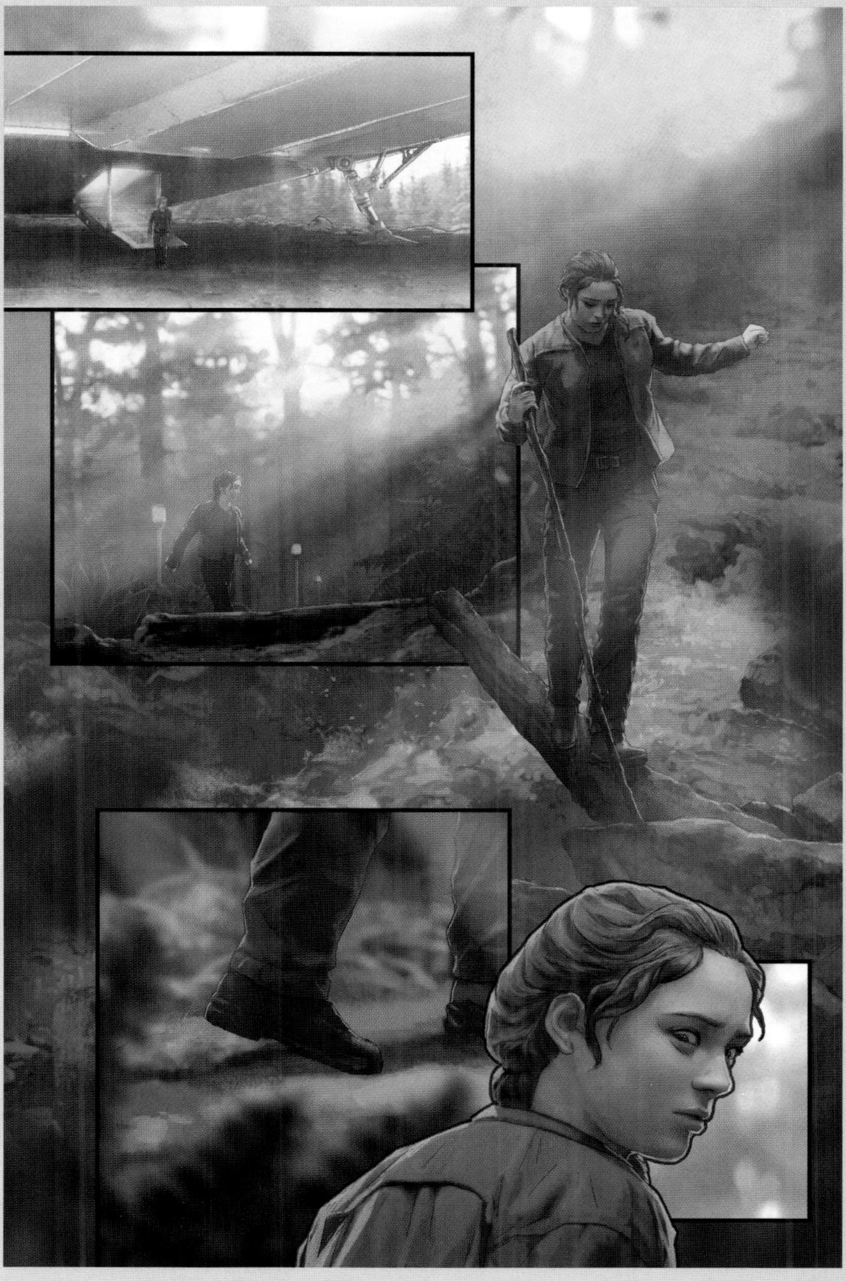

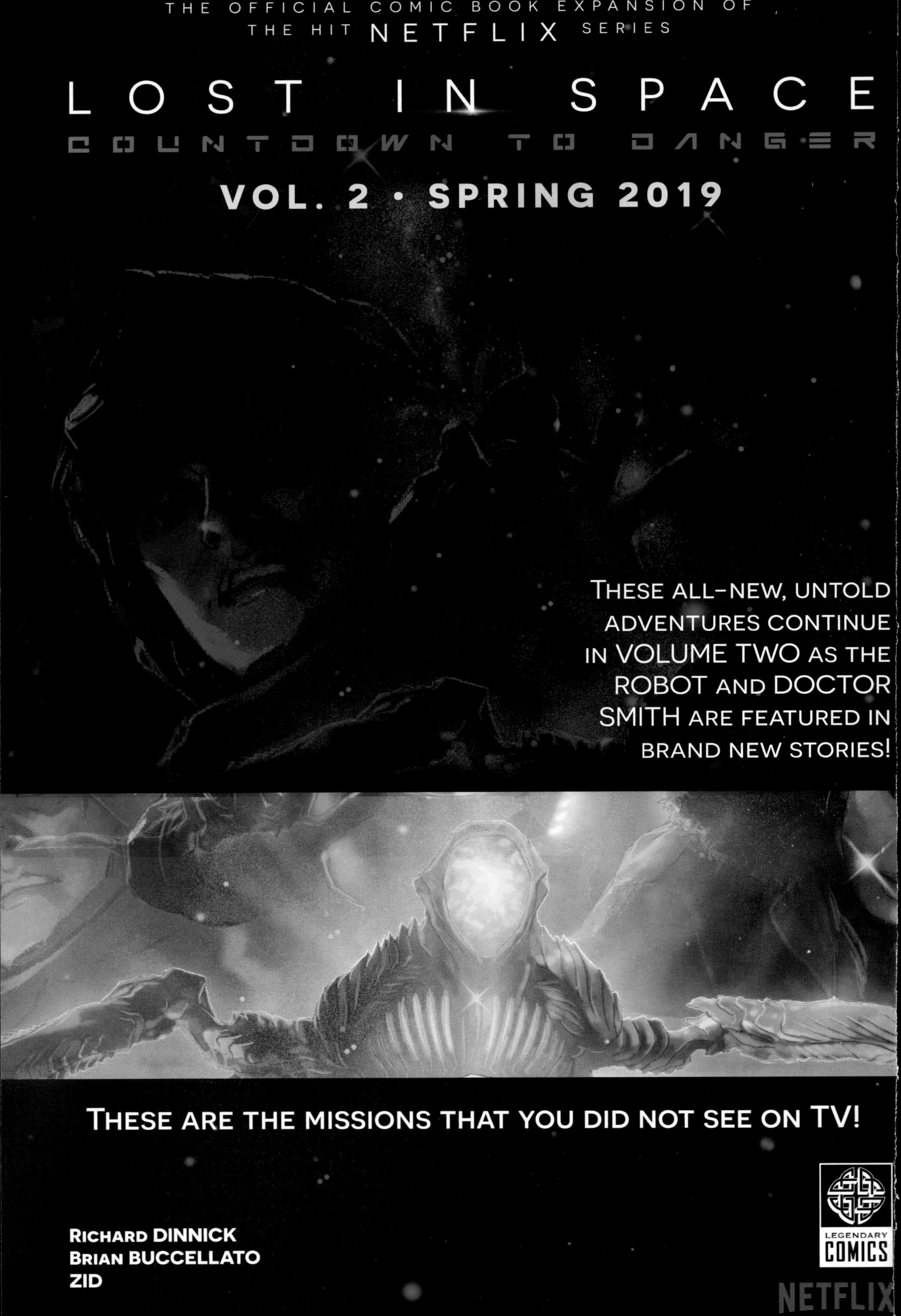
THE OFFICIAL COMIC BOOK EXPANSION OF
THE HIT NETFLIX SERIES
LOST IN SPACE
COUNTDOWN TO DANGER
VOL. 2 • SPRING 2019
THESE ALL-NEW, UNTOLD ADVENTURES CONTINUE IN VOLUME TWO AS THE ROBOT AND DOCTOR SMITH ARE FEATURED IN BRAND NEW STORIES!
THESE ARE THE MISSIONS THAT YOU DID NOT SEE ON TV!
RICHARD DINNICK
BRIAN BUCCELLATO
ZID
LEGENDARY COMICS
NETFLIX

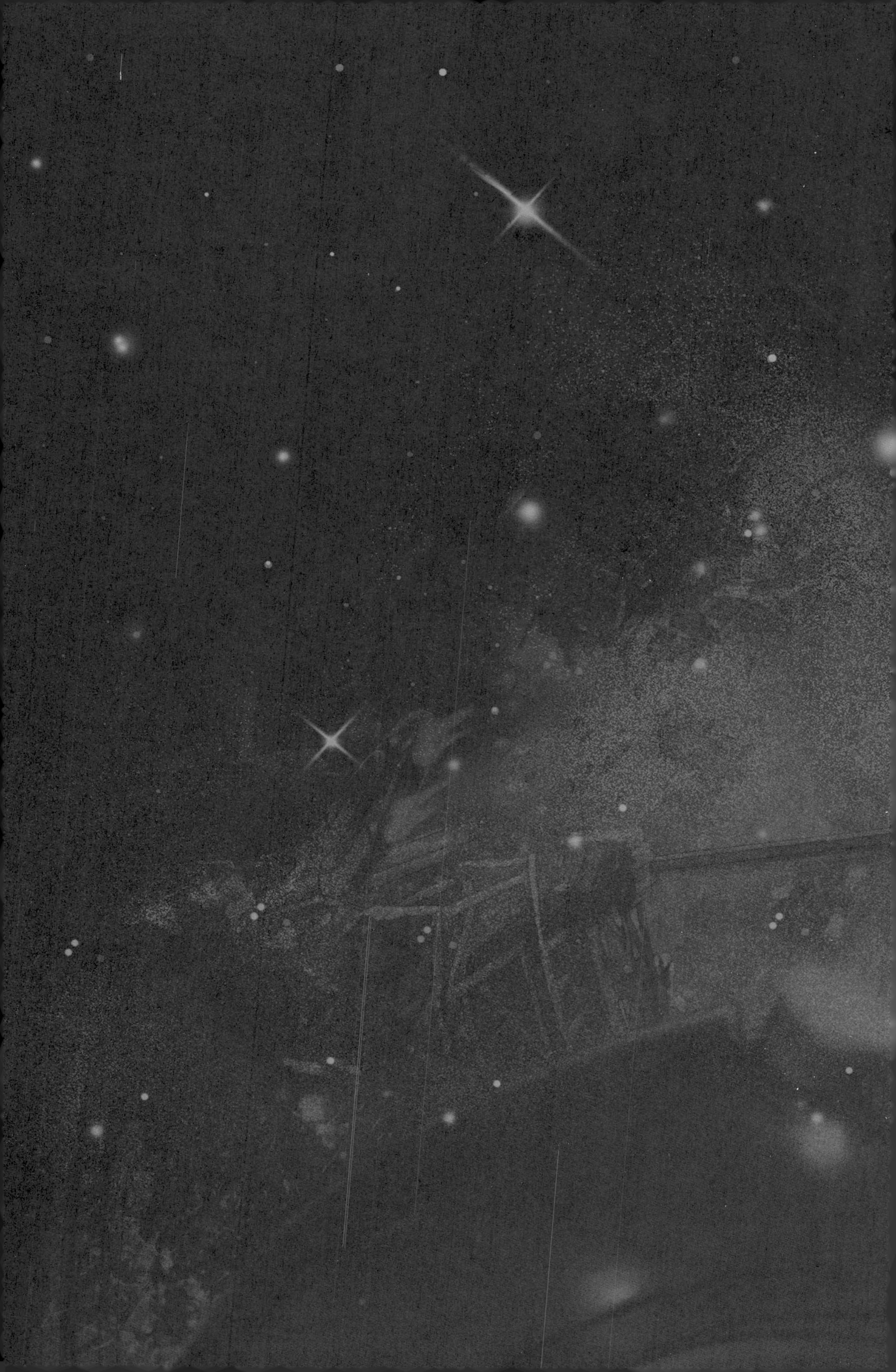